TABLE OF CONTENTS

ACRONYMS

CJCS	Chairman of the Joint Chiefs of Staff
DPRK	Democratic Peoples Republic of Korea
EU	European Union
GWOT	Global War on Terror
IAEA	International Atomic Energy Agency
ICBM	Inter-Continental Ballistic Missile
IDF	Israeli Defense Forces
IRGC	Iranian Revolutionary Guard Corps
NBC	Nuclear, Biological, and Chemical
NMS	National Military Strategy
NPT	Nuclear Non-Proliferation Treaty
NSCT	National Strategy for Combating Terrorism
NSS	National Security Strategy
PLO	Palestinian Liberation Organization
PSI	Proliferation Security Initiative
UNEF	United Nations Emergency Force
UNIFIL	United Nations Interim Force in Lebanon
UNMOVIC	United Nations Monitoring, Verification and Inspection Commission
UNSCOM	United Nations Special Committee
UNSCR	United Nations Security Council Resolution
WMD	Weapons of Mass Destruction

ILLUSTRATIONS

TABLES

CHAPTER 1

INTRODUCTION

> That one should never allow chaos to develop in order to avoid
> going to war, because one does not avoid a war but instead puts it
> off to his disadvantage.

Machiavelli, *The Prince*

At 6:00 A.M., Friday, 21 March 2003, four divisions, three American and one

British, crossed the Iraqi Border in a long postponed drive to topple Saddam Hussein.

Arguably, this was the final act of the 1991 Gulf War, when a coalition led by the United

States had driven Saddam Hussein's invasion force from Kuwait. However, many saw

this as the first example of the United States' new policy of preemptive war promulgated

in the *National Security Strategy* (*NSS*) of 2002. The resulting considerable confusion

over the policy of preemption is partially related to the timing of its publishing because of

the parallel buildup of offensive capability aimed at Saddam Hussein and Iraq. As a

result, Iraq became an example of an illegal war based on the immoral doctrine of

preemption for many opposed to the war in the United States and especially Europe.

Contributing to this argument is the confusion over the definitions of preemptive war,

preventive war, wars of aggression, and continuations of hostilities. Even though the war

against Saddam, which constituted Operation Iraqi Freedom-1, resulted in a decisive

military victory, the war against the terrorists and insurgents in Iraq, and globally, is far

from over. What defined the type of war against Iraq also clarifies the type of war that the

United States is fighting in the overall Global War on Terror (GWOT). It will be one of

long periods of military action by one or the other side with no initiation of hostilities in

the formal sense, for example, Declaration of War, or termination of hostilities by some

1

form of peace accord. In this context, words matter and how those words are defined mean the difference between building effective coalitions of the willing and the perception that the United States is again playing the cowboy in unilateral action.

With this in mind, what are the implications on international relations of the United States adopting a preemptive strategy? To formulate an answer, this thesis will explore the following questions; what is the definition of preemptive war? Are there criteria for establishing a credible basis for the use of preemptive force? Is there historical precedence for preemptive war? Was the United States attack on Iraq in 2003 an example of a preemptive strategy? Does the strategy towards Iraq set precedent for the GWOT? Finally, what are the implications of a preemptive strategy for the GWOT? In order to understand the establishment of preemption as a cornerstone of the *NSS* of 2002, the circumstances that led up to its adoption must be explored.

Background

The events of 11 September 2001 were a wake up call to the United States. The expected enemy, Saddam Hussein, was suddenly and violently, if temporarily, substituted by "shadowy networks of individuals" (*NSS* 2002, 2). This new enemy differed in that it also was not a state. It owned no territory and was responsible to no constituency. In short, there was no central point for the United States to attack, no easily identifiable centers of gravity on which to focus its prodigious elements of state power. These terrorists, who had demonstrated no compunction against killing thousands in the World Trade Center, would not be limited in the means of attack by United States threats to retaliate in kind. However, where would the United States retaliate and against whom? Similar threats had appeared successful in persuading Saddam Hussein not to use weapons of mass destruction (WMD) in the first Gulf War. However, it seemed well within the realm of possibility, even a probability, that the terrorists would use WMD against the United States. President Bush responded to this threat in the *NSS* of 2002,

> The gravest danger our nation faces lies at the crossroads of radicalism and technology. Our enemies have openly declared that they are seeking weapons of mass destruction, and evidence indicates that they are doing so with determination. The United States will not allow these efforts to succeed . . . as a matter of common sense and self-defense, America will act against such emerging threats before they are fully formed. (*NSS* 2002, 3)

The *NSS* lays out the policy of attacking these "emerging threats before they are fully formed." It lays out the United States' adoption of the policy of preemption as an integral part of self-defense. It is also a complete break with the strategies of deterrence and containment that had been the driving concepts behind United States national security policy since the beginning of the cold war, over fifty years ago. However, what is preemption and why is it important for the United States?

Simply put, "A preemptive strike occurs when war is imminent" (Nye 2003, 157). A policy of preemption means that when a state "B" threatens state "A" with "imminent" attack, state A may strike state B first. It is a proactive self-defense. However, it is not a simple policy, and it is fraught with controversy. Just as beauty is in the eye of the beholder so is the concept of imminence. In this case, state B may be rattling its saber with no real intent to attack state A. State A, having no way to determine this, may consider itself the subject of a real attack and respond appropriately in legitimate self-defense. It also means that a state may attack another nation without declaring war. This is in direct conflict with traditional notions of declaring war prior to the actual commencement of hostilities. In the Peloponnesian War, the city-state of Corinth prepared to march against Corcyra (modern-day Corfu). Corcyra proposed terms to avert war, however,

> None of these proposals were acceptable to the Corinthians. By this time, their ships were manned and their allies were ready. *They sent in front of them a Herald to declare war* [emphasis mine], and then set sail with a force of seventy-five ships and 2,000 hoplites to fight against the Corcyraeans at Epidamnus. (Thucydides 1972, 52)

In accordance with accepted norms of international behavior, the Corinthians notified the Corcyraeans that they were declaring war before setting sail. This norm remains in effect today. The United States, itself, with great indignation condemned the Japanese attack on Pearl Harbor prior to a declaration of war. The Japanese attack on Pearl Harbor was not by definition preemption, however, but comparisons highlight the significant confusion over what that definition is and how it differs from preventive war that adds to the controversy. However, the problem with preemption as an announced policy is not necessarily the act of preemption itself. The problem is how the international community views the act, itself. Nations have rarely, if ever, knowingly allowed other nations to attack them first militarily. In effect, to be legitimate the causal factors behind the attack must be explained to the international community and the international community must agree to support, or tolerate, the action taken.

Driving the adoption of preemption as policy is the exponential increase in technology that is available to the modern terrorist. Technology now allows the terrorist to plan, coordinate, and execute attacks on a scale unimagined prior to 11 September. Even worse, it potentially enables the terrorist to employ WMD. The effects of which, as a terrorist weapon, would also be on a scale unimagined prior to 11 September. It is no longer a question of only planeloads of people but the devastation of entire cities and regions.

The *NSS* is the document that sets the direction for all of the departments in the Executive Branch of the United States Government. It also spawns guidance and direction from each of those departments, such as the Departments of Defense' National Military Strategy (NMS), which further defines planning, programs, and expenditures for their subordinate departments and elements. The *NSS* of 2002 marked a significant departure from the policy since the end of World War II for two reasons. First, previous policies had been aimed at states. Second, those same previous policies were meant to deter the enemy by the maintenance of significant force. The 11th of September had turned this policy on its head. The enemy was now shadowy networks of individuals, not states, and deterrence was not effective, as 11 September seemed to exemplify. While it had always maintained the right to self-defense, this national security policy clearly articulated a new policy of preemption associated with the right to self-defense. Instead of waiting while an enemy prepares to strike a blow against the interests of the United States, now it is a matter of policy to strike first against that same enemy.

The *NSS* resulted in significant controversy both here in the Unites States and throughout the international community. There are three main reasons for this controversy. The first reason is the problem of definitions as discussed previously in this research. The second reason is the timing of the release of the new *NSS*. The President released the policy after the successful intervention in Afghanistan and during, what is now known to be, the build-up to war in Iraq. Finally, the *NSS* document itself uses the words preemptive and preventive interchangeably, even though both words have separate

5

and distinct meanings in the lexicon of international affairs. As the capstone document for the United States Government, this confusion has far-reaching implications because it is the guidance used to determine policy at all subordinate levels, including operational and budgetary planning.

The *NMS* of 2004, which cites details this in the introduction, "The 2004 NMS supports the NSS by establishing a set of overarching defense objectives that guide the Department's security activities and provide direction for the National Military Strategy" (*NMS* 2004, 1).

As does the *National Strategy for Combating Terrorism* (*NSCT*), "This combating terrorism strategy further elaborates on Section III of the National Security Strategy by expounding on our need to destroy terrorist organizations, 'win the war of ideas,' and strengthens America's security at home and abroad" (*NSCT* 2003, 2). The *NSS* sets in motion millions of people and billions of dollars worth of expenditures to meet the objectives it lays out. That is why it is important to understand the strategy of preemption as a pillar of the current *NSS*.

It is also important to look at and evaluate domestic and international reaction to the United States' adoption of the policy of preemption as an integral component of the *NSS*. Many people inside the United States and internationally regard the adoption of preemption as an illegal and immoral policy that authorizes one state to attack another without provocation. This is an oversimplification. National leaders, generally, charged with the responsibility of their people and homelands, act out of national interest and not "whim." In fairness to other nations, it is generally not in their interest to have other nations publicly state that they will fire the first shot, so to speak, whenever they feel their interests threatened. This refers back to Yoram Dinstein and the concept of imminence. In the United States, a country that has a long and generally beneficent history of antimilitarism, the policy of preemption seems to indicate the adoption of an extreme interventionist position.

In order to evaluate the United States' policy of preemption, as delineated in the *NSS* of 2002, and whether the international and domestic objections are valid, three case studies will be examined. Each of these cases involves the military actions of Israel in what might be termed preemptive attacks. They are:

1. The Arab-Israeli War of 1967.

2. The Israeli strike on the Iraqi nuclear reactor at the Al Tuwaitha Nuclear Center in 1981 (Osirak).

3. The Israeli invasion of Lebanon in 1982.

Each of these case studies highlights the reasons behind the interventions and their legality. They also relate directly to what the United States is now facing in its war against the shadowy network of individuals. The 1967 war case study is preemption in its clearest form. State A, Israel, suspecting an imminent attack by state B, Egypt, reacts to the threat by striking the first blow and devastating state, B's war making capability. The second case study involves the actions of one state when it believed that it faced a clear nuclear threat. The third case study is an examination of a state conducting antiterrorist operations by invading a third-party country in order to deny their enemy sanctuaries. Israeli military history is not the subject of this thesis, but the political circumstances, either international or domestic, that drove them to take these actions are relevant to the discussion of preemption and the reaction of the international community, including the

United States, is instructive for the future of United States policy. The Israeli example and the resulting international isolation resulting from their actions in these case studies are indicative of the reaction to be expected from the international community when and if the United States engages in preemptive attacks. These examples also lend themselves to review because they are controversial and set international legal precedents that are relevant to the adoption and execution of the *NSS* policy of preemption.

Once the factors involved in the Israeli case studies are examined. The same process will used to evaluate three possible cases of preemption in United States Foreign Policy. One of which, Iraq, is now historical, but the other two, Iran and North Korea, are possible future scenarios in which the United States may execute a preemptive strategy.

1. The 2003 Invasion of Iraq.

2. Preemptive attack on North Korea.

3. Preemptive attack on Iran.

As in Israeli case studies, each of the United States case studies considers conventional attack, terrorist attack, and the potential use of WMD by either rogue states or terrorists. The potential for legitimacy or for international isolation and the resulting effect on future United States foreign policy is the focus of these case studies

Definitions

Where does a strategy of preemption fit into other warlike acts such as wars of aggression, preventive war, and wars resulting from preexisting hostilities? Aggression is defined as: "Any use of force or imminent threat of force by one state against the political sovereignty or territorial integrity of another constitutes aggression and is a criminal act" (Walzer 2000, 62). A war of aggression is then a state that uses force "against the

8

political sovereignty or territorial integrity of another." For example, Iraq's unprovoked attack on Kuwait in 1991 is thus a war of aggression and was found to be so by the United States Congress in a joint resolution authorizing the use of force against Iraq.

The definition of a preventive war is a war that "occurs when statesmen believe merely that war is better now than later" (Nye 2003, 157). The Japanese attack on Pearl Harbor fits this category. The Japanese attacked, not because the United States was preparing to attack Japan, but because the United States might later attack, in response to the Japanese attack on British and French colonial possession in the Pacific or interfere with the transport of resources from those colonies to the home islands. The key consideration in preventive war is that the attacked state does not have to be actively preparing for war only that they might be at some later, unspecified time.

A war resulting from preexisting hostilities is really an extension of an earlier war that had no formal or informal conclusion. This is not a reference to a conflict that may trace its beginning to the unsatisfactory or unsuccessful conclusion of an earlier war, such as is often quoted about World War II growing out of the aftermath of World War I. World War I had various treaties signed by both Allied and German representatives that officially concluded the hostilities. A war growing out of preexisting hostilities is a conflict where one belligerent party fails to comply with the terms of a cease-fire and prior to the conclusion of a peace treaty.

> The suspension of hostilities must not be confused with their cessation. A cessation of hostilities means that the war is over. A suspension of hostilities connotes that the state of war goes on, but temporarily there is no actual warfare. (Dinstein 2001, 54)

Thus the war has not ended, regardless of the length of time between the cease-fire and the violation of that cease-fire.

A war of preemption is, as mentioned earlier, a form of pro-active self-defense, for definitions sake "A preemptive strike occurs when war is imminent" (Nye 2003, 157). In short, a state may defend its "political sovereignty and territorial integrity" and not wait for an aggressor nation to cross its borders or attack its citizens. The challenge is in a subjective determination of what imminent means. If state A is building up its forces for an exercise along the border of state B, and state B believes that this is actually preparatory to an attack, state B has the right to defend itself. However, if state B is only conducting exercises to "rattle the saber" and intimidate state A, does state A still have the right to attack state B? Why would the United States adopt a policy that is as nebulous and controversial as preemption to justify military strikes?

Central to the legal definition of preemption is the Caroline Case of 1842. The Caroline was a ship in United States waters suspected by the British authorities in Canada of being used to support Canadian rebels. The British attacked and destroyed the vessel despite its location. In response, the United States Secretary of State, Daniel Webster wrote, "there must be shown 'a necessity of self-defense . . . instant, overwhelming, leaving no choice for means and no moment for deliberation'" (Walzer 2000, 74). It is from this case that the three criteria for preemption derive immediacy, proportionality, and necessity (Dinstein 2001, 219).

Just War as a theory has its roots in writings of Saint Augustine and Saint Thomas Aquinas. Saint Augustine stipulated that though war is "lamentable" it could be necessary to right a "wrong suffered at the hands of an adversary." Saint Thomas Aquinas further delineated a "just war" by requiring that it "fulfill three conditions: (i) the war had to be conducted not privately but under the authority of a prince (*auctoritas principis*); (ii)

10

there had to be a 'just cause' (*causa justa*) for the war; and (iii) it was not enough t have a just cause from an objective viewpoint, but it was necessary to have the right intention (*intentio recta*) to promote good and to avoid evil" (Dinstein 2001, 60).

Limitations

Throughout history, there are numerous examples of nations taking action that are preemptive. However, in the interests of clarity and brevity, this thesis will limit itself to Israel in three historical case studies exhibiting characteristics that directly relate to the threats currently faced by the United States and that the *NSS* of 2002 specifically addresses.

For the purposes of these case studies, this thesis will restrict itself to the five permanent members of the United Nations Security Council as a barometer of world opinion and legitimacy. The Security Council has the legal authority, granted by the United Nations under Article 51 of the Charter, to take "measures necessary to maintain international peace and security" (Gray 2000, 88). This is one of the key exceptions to the prohibitions of the use of force; the other is the right to self-defense. To authorize, or acquiesce, to any use of force requires the five permanent members of the council to, at the minimum, abstain from exercising their veto power. Even if every other member of the Security Council votes for a resolution that accepts or condemns a particular use of force, just one permanent member can cause the Security Council to reject the resolution by exercising its veto power.

Significance of the Study

With the reelection of George W. Bush as President of the United States,

preemption is likely to remain a cornerstone of United States' policy as stated in the *NSS*,

"While the United States will constantly strive to enlist the support of the International

community, we will not hesitate to act alone, if necessary to exercise our right of self-

defense by acting preemptively against such terrorists, to prevent them from doing harm

against our people and country" (2002, 6).

This is a concern even of America's strongest allies in the world, because it

appears to confirm a unilateralist policy by the United States and opens a pandora's box

in setting a precedent for other less scrupulous nations. Concerning the unilateralist

policy critique, the *NSS* goes to great lengths to emphasize that it will work with the

international community as stated in the above quote. However, the Pandora's Box

already seems to be a valid argument. In 2002, President Putin of Russia made threats to

attack into Georgia in order "to prevent Chechen 'bandits' from launching raids into

Chechnya. Putin cited the UN charter--specifically, the provisions concerning the right of

self-defense, to support his tough stance on Georgia" (Torbakov 2002, 1). In the

aftermath of the Chechen attack on Beslan, Russia also seems to have adopted a policy of

preemption,

> Russian statements this week by the chief of the Armed Forces General Staff and
> Defense Minister Sergei Ivanov followed the terrorist incident at a school in
> North Ossetia in which nearly 350 people were killed. Ivanov reiterated yesterday
> that Russia has the right to make preemptive strikes against terrorists at home and
> abroad. Prior to the statements, the Kremlin had updated its military protocol to
> allow for preventive strikes. (McMahon 2004)

Australia's Prime Minister, John Howard, has even indicated a willingness to use

preemptive action against terrorists if necessary. "It stands to reason that if you believe that somebody was going to launch an attack on your country . . . and you had a capacity to stop it, and there was no alternative other than to use that capacity, then of course you would have to use it" (Murphy 2002). His definition closely resembles that spelled out by Nye.

The United States faces two possibilities that might warrant the exercise of a preemptive attack, rogue nations and terrorists. At the top of the list for rogue nations are Iran and North Korea. Both states are possibly developing the capability to build WMD; North Korea claims to have already succeeded in building a bomb. Iran's stated position is that their development of nuclear potential is for the sole purpose of generating power not weapons development. Except for a brief period, their failure to allow inspection by the International Atomic Energy Agency (IAEA) undermines their credibility as does their anti-United States and Israel rhetoric. North Korea has already demonstrated the capability to reach Japan with their No-Dong missiles and they refused inspection of their developing nuclear power plants. Both their rhetoric and policy maintain that they are constantly under imminent threat of attack by the United States. North Korea and Iran are states with readily identifiable infrastructure and territory to strike that gives the United States some capability to deter rogue actions but as noted earlier, the terrorists do not.

That means, just as in the case studies on Lebanon in 1982 and not as in Iraq in 2003, the United States will have to violate the territorial integrity and political sovereignty of a third-party nation to strike at the terrorists. The implications are staggering, even if the environment is permissive. If the environment were non-permissive, as in both case studies, then that would mean a war against the third party state that is willingly, or unwillingly, harboring the terrorist cell. In short the United

States would fight its way in, just to fight the terrorists, and then fight its way out again.

CHAPTER 2

LITERATURE REVIEW

We must take the battle to the enemy, disrupt his plans and confront the worst threats before they emerge. In the world we have entered, the only path to safety is the path of action. And this nation will act. (2002)

President George W. Bush

Introduction

Preemption is not a new concept, but its inclusion in President George W. Bush's *NSS* of 2002 has rejuvenated the controversy over preemption as a strategy. The controversy stems from a perceived "broadening the meaning to encompass preventive war" (O'Hanlon et al. 2002, 1). This document produced a ripple affect throughout the world that has resulted in the publishing of dozens of articles on the subject. In the context of the United States Government, the *NSS* is the capstone document from which all-subordinate policies and directives derive their guidance and direction. As a result, the *NSS* of 2002 spawned multiple documents from different departments and agencies further clarifying their roles and responsibilities under the stated national security policy of the Bush administration, specifically recognizing preemption as a cornerstone of that policy. The reaction, both domestically and internationally, directly resulted in a tremendous abundance of newspaper and journal articles both attacking and defending preemption as an appropriate policy for international relations. Additionally, it has also been the subject of numerous studies from think tanks and the subject of multiple scholarly theses from war colleges, defense universities, all discussing the impact and execution of such a policy.

The *NSS* had four primary themes. "assure our allies and friends; dissuade future military competition; deter threats against U.S. interests; and decisively defeat any adversary if deterrence fails" (2002, 29). Assure, dissuade, deter, and defeat; but it also claimed "as a matter of common sense and self-defense, America will act against such emerging threats before they are fully formed" (*NSS* 2002, v). In short, the Bush administration asserted the strategy of preemption, or anticipatory self-defense, not only against terrorists but also "will hold to account nations that are compromised by terror, including those who harbor terrorists" (*NSS* 2002, iv-v). However, the document makes no distinction between preemption and prevention; indeed it uses them interchangeably and thereby muddles its own assertion and the legality of such an act.

> The United States has long maintained the option of preemptive actions to counter a sufficient threat to our national security. The greater the threat, the greater is the risk of inaction--and the more compelling the case for taking anticipatory action to defend ourselves, even if uncertainty remains as to the time and place of the enemy's attack. To forestall or prevent such hostile acts by our adversaries, the United States will, if necessary, act preemptively. (*NSS* 2002, 15)

In fact in the preceding paragraphs, the document attempts to widen the definition of preemption on the assumption that terrorists and rogue nations will not comply, even determinedly seek to avoid, traditional indicators of an attack.

> Legal scholars and international jurists often conditioned the legitimacy of preemption on the existence of an imminent threat--most often a visible mobilization of armies, navies, and air forces preparing to attack. We must adapt the concept of an imminent threat to the capabilities and objectives of today's adversaries. Rogue states and terrorists do not seek to attack us using conventional means. They know such attacks would fail. Instead, they rely on acts of terror and, potentially, the use of weapons of mass destruction--weapons that can be easily concealed, delivered covertly, and used without warning. (*NSS* 2002, 15)

This adaptation to the new threat of terrorist and rogue nations is more in line with Michael N. Schmitt's concept of "last window of opportunity" discussed later.

16

The 17 June 2003, Report of the Task Force on Peace and Security by the United Nations Association, National Capital Area entitled, *The U.S. Doctrine of Preemptive Attack: Real Problem, Wrong Answer* takes the view the Bush administration's strategy is preventive rather than preemptive and questions the imminence of any attack using WMD on the United States.

> The administration designates this policy as "preemptive," a word that normally refers to actions designed to head off a pending or imminent attack that has already taken definite form. We share the view of several commentators who suggest that the right term for this policy should not be preemptive but "preventive" action. (Dean 2003, 2)

This has negative international consequences for the United States relating to the illegality of preventive war vice the legality of preemptive war and contributes to a credibility gap for American Foreign Policy. The credibility gap had tangible repercussions in the limited support demonstrated, and even offered, for the United States' attack on Iraq in 2003 in complete contrast to the support shown after Iraq invaded Kuwait in 1991 (Dean 2003, 4).

Despite the *NSS*'s assertion that preemption has always been an option for the United States, Christopher S. Owens in "Unlikely Partners: Preemption and the American Way of War" proposes that a preemptive strategy "is a departure from the traditional American way of war" (Owens 2003, 2). He defines the "traditional" as the United States having a "reputation for its willingness to defend itself abroad only after receiving the enemy's first assault" (Owens 2003, 8). This assertion itself is debatable and hardly addresses the hundreds of interventions as a result of threats, or perceived threats, to United States interests. With that said, however, he also emphasizes that having a preemptive strategy, feasible and creditable, can be a deterrent to those rogue states and

17

terrorists, "determined adversaries" (Owens 2003, 14). Instead of a separate strategy, preemption falls more properly under the construct of the *NSS*'s concept of "deter threats against U.S. interests" (*NSS* 2002, 29).

The *NMS* of 2004 conveys the vision of the Chairman of the Joint Chiefs of Staff (CJCS) on how to support the *NSS* and the *NDS* of 2004. In it the CJCS applies the tenets laid out in the *NSS* to the military element of power. "The National Military Strategy is guided by the goals and objectives contained in the President's National Security Strategy and serves to implement the Secretary of Defense's 2004 National Military Strategy of The United States of America" (*NMS*, iv).

The CJCS lays out three objectives in *NMS:*

1. Protect the United States.

2. Prevent conflict and surprise attack.

3. Prevail against adversaries (2004, 2).

These objectives reflect the disaster of 11 September 2001, and are clearly different from the "shape respond, and prepare now" of the previous administrations 1997 *NMS*. The tense used implies immediacy as opposed to the earlier *NMS* objectives, which tense implies distance and time from action. The difference between the two is the difference between a pre-11 September and a post-11 September global strategy.

However the *NMS* of 2004 also reflects the ambiguity of the *NSS* over the difference between a preemptive strategy and preventive war. It places the logical basis for a preemptive military strategy squarely under the second objective of preventing conflict and surprise attack. "The potentially catastrophic impact of an attack against the United States, its allies, and its interests may necessitate actions in self-defense to preempt adversaries before they can attack" (*NMS* 2004, 2). The word preempt itself is used as a synonym for attack in this passage, but what is even more confusing is that preemption is by Nye's definition, self-defense against adversaries before they can attack. This significantly lowers the general nature of preemption to that of a mere spoiling attack and not a deliberate political decision.

The introduction of the role of combatant commander's into the national military strategy further obscures the issue. "*When directed* [Emphasis mine] commanders will preempt in self-defense those adversaries that pose an unmistakable threat of grave harm and which are not otherwise deterrable" (*NMS* 2004, 8). The phrase, when directed, flies completely in the face of Daniel Webster's "instant, overwhelming, leaving no choice of means, and no moment for deliberation" (Dinstein 2001, 219). On the contrary, when directed implies that there is time to evaluate the situation and report to higher headquarters vice taking instant steps to counter an impending threat. Again, preempt is seemingly used as a synonym for the word attack. The following phrase "in self-defense" is superfluous because, once again, by definition to conduct a preemptive strike incorporates the requirement of self-defense. If regional combatant commanders are going to execute the preemptive strategy directed by the NMS, then the nature of the guidance given to them must be more general than specific in nature.

Also included in the *NMS* 2004 is a passage on preventing surprise attacks, which establishes a policy of "preventative missions on time critical targets using coordinated efforts with other agencies and departments in the US Government" (*NMS* 2004, 12). In short, the CJCS has laid out a preventive war strategy and blurred the lines between preemptive and preventive strikes.

19

The *NSCT*, issued by the White House, is a comprehensive look at attacking

terrorists across all of the elements of power. In introducing the 4D strategy of:

1. Defeat terrorist organizations.
2. Deny further sponsorship support and sanctuary.
3. Diminish the underlying causes.
4. Defend the United States. (*NSCT* 2003, 11-12)

The Bush administration attempts to define the operating environment and synchronize

the efforts of all federal agencies in the GWOT. It also emphasizes in contradiction to the

NMS 1997 that the United States cannot afford a strategy that responds to terrorism. This

clearly implies the need to seek out and preempt terrorist attacks. It also emphasizes the

need to deal with states that support, willingly or not, terrorists to operate within their

borders. "Where states are unwilling, we will act decisively to counter the threat they

pose and, ultimately, to compel them to cease supporting terrorism" (*NSCT* 2003, 12).

This is the younger Bush's "line in the sand," so to speak, and a clear challenge to the

world to choose sides. But it is also a concept supported by the International Court of

Justice in the Corfu Channel Case, "that every State is under an obligation not to allow

knowingly its territory to be used for acts contrary to the rights of other states" (Dinstein

2001, 214). States that allow terrorists to use their territory as sanctuaries or staging bases

then tacitly agree to, indeed, require other states to do for that nation hat it cannot do for

itself. This is the same argument that Secretary of State, John Quincy Adams, made in

response to Spanish protestations when General Andrew Jackson invaded Florida in

1818. "That Spain's failure to preserve order along the borderlands justified preemptive

American action" (Leffler 2004, 23). Preemptive action as opposed to preventive action

has a long legally justified, history.

Both the *NMS* and the *NSCT* reflect the guidance established by the *NSS* of 2002. The *NSCT* 4D strategy and the *NMS* three objectives are complementary in character. But they also reflect the confusion over preemptive strike and preventive war. Both state the necessity for allies to provide bases, support and forces for the war on terror, but they both also stress the possibility of unilateral action if required. A stated policy of unilateralism may seem strong but it wards off the very allies both documents say they need. The *NSCT* specifically discusses the need to win the war of ideas by equating terrorism with slavery, piracy, and genocide, in the lexicon of international relations (*NSCT* 2003, 23-24). However, on the next page it notes the damaging effect that the Israeli-Palestinian conflict has on United States foreign relations in the Middle East but then absolves itself of any responsibility by stating that only the Palestinians and the Israelis can end the conflict.

The strategy of preemption, itself, falls into the greater context of the development of international law and custom in regards to war and hostilities. The context of international law is what give, or denies, legitimacy in the eyes of the world to strategy. Legitimacy is of primary importance because of the increasing interconnection of states due to technology. "If a state's acts are perceived as illegitimate, the costs of a policy will be higher. States appeal to international law and organization to legitimize their own policies or to delegitimize others, and that often shapes their tactics and outcomes" (Nye 2003, 164). What takes place in one hemisphere is no longer isolated from the rest of the world and the establishment of United Nations has given an equal voice, if not influence, to even the smallest nation in terms of size, population, economic, or military power. There are numerous works on international law both in book form and

21

in the aforementioned newspaper and journal articles. With certain significant exceptions, this research will draw on only the most recent interpretive works. Finally, multiple resolutions of the United Nations Security Council will be included to explore the legitimacy of action taken by belligerents in the course of conducting international relations.

The literature review is organized according to how the resources address the subordinate and tertiary questions. The focus of the review is on the assertions each resource makes, the evidence provided to support the assertion(s) and the validity of the assertion(s). The review will be further organized parallel to the thesis overall, beginning with the general in defining preemption and the policy of the United States Government to the specific in reference to the case studies, analysis, and finally conclusions to be drawn.

Subordinate Question 1: What is the definition of Preemptive War? In order to understand the ramifications of the inclusion preemption in the *NSS* of 2002, the legal and theoretical basis for the concept of preemption must first be understood. This is a critical aspect of the question, because a large portion of the printed discussion available today is confusing, often using the phrase preemptive war as a synonym for the concept of preventive war. As mentioned earlier, this conflict is found even in the *NSS* of 2002, where preemption and prevention are regarded as almost interchangeable concepts. The following authors clarify the distinction in definition and provide the necessary legal and theoretical basis for understanding the impact of a preemptive strategy in international relations.

Joseph Nye's *Understanding International Conflicts: An Introduction to Theory and History* is an introduction to concepts of strategy with the primary purpose of providing the student "with conceptual tools that will help them shape their own answers as the future unfolds" (Nye 2003, xi). He advances general concepts but does not make judgments on those same concepts including the definitions of preemptive and preventive war that he provides. It is Nye's definitions of preemptive and preventive wars that will be used in this work. His definitions are as follows, "A preemptive strike occurs when war is imminent. A preventive war occurs when statesmen believe merely that war is better now than later" (2003, 157). The distinction between preemptive and preventive is that of time or imminence and is critical because of the legal ramifications. A preemptive strike is self-defense and therefore legal. A preventive strike is aggression and thereby illegal, with all of the consequences that illegal acts entail in the international community.

Yoram Dinstein in *War, Aggression and Self-Defence* provides a more detailed framework for the use of force in international relations. He traces the legal basis of international conflicts in contrast to "a general reference to international armed conflicts ignores the important theoretical as well as practical distinctions existing between wars and other uses of inter-state force (short of war)" (2001, xii). He does not use the word preemption but instead uses anticipatory self-defense in the same context. Dinstein lays out the acceptable criteria for preemptive action laid out by Daniels Webster in the Caroline Case: specifically necessity, proportionality, and immediacy. He explores the concept of self-defense in international affairs; its impact in history, and the current impact including Kosovo in the updated edition.

Michael Walzer's *Just and Unjust Wars* uses legal precepts but applies moral conditions to the use of force. Where Dinstein looks to international law to decide the appropriateness of state action, Walzer looks to international law to support the morality of state action. Joseph Nye identifies Walzer as a "state moralist" for whom "intervention is rarely justified" (Nye 2003, 157). Significantly, Dinstein is an Israeli and was a Professor of International Law at Tel Aviv University when the first edition of this work was published in 1988. Walzer's work, however, was first published in the United States in 1977, a period of remarkable political turmoil and heightened anti-interventionism. Walzer also takes issue with Webster's criteria of immediacy not as an unwarranted element but because he believes that states will have the time to effect settlement by more peaceful means instead of resorting to force. However, Walzer's book is often referenced as a seminal work on morality in international relations.

An important theoretician on the concept of preemption is Michael N. Schmitt who has written extensively on the use of force in international relations in general, and preemption specifically, including *Counter-Terrorism and the Use of Force in International Law*, from the George C. Marshall European Center for Security Studies, and "Preemptive Strategies in International Law" published in the *Michigan Journal of International Law*. The latter is particularly important because it introduces and explains the concept of "window of opportunity." Window of opportunity is an expansion of Webster's criteria of immediacy as applied to terrorist attacks. In short, the only window of opportunity that exists to prevent a terrorist attack may be "long before a planned attack" (Schmitt 2003b, 534). In contrast, Michael O'Hanlon, Susan E. Rice, and James B. Steinberg in Policy Brief #113: *The New National Security Strategy and Preemption*, published by the Brookings Institution assert that terrorists "groups' past practices and explicit statements provide an adequate substitute for the traditional doctrine's requirement for imminent threat" (2002, 5). In short, the criterion to be met for immediacy to act against terrorists currently exists and is provided by the terrorists themselves.

With the basis set for an understanding of the concept and legal context of preemption as a strategy, it is important to look to its adoption as policy. President Bush's administration included preemption as a key element of *NSS of the United States of America,* September 2002. This document is the capstone document that theoretically provides direction and guidance to subordinate elements of the United States Government. It is also extremely controversial because of its inclusion of preemption, a strategy that too many threatens the Westphalian construct of the nature of states and state interaction. Paradoxically, it is seen by some as more of a threat than that which it was designed to fight international terrorism. Direct lines can be drawn from the *NSS,* September 2002 to the following subordinate policy documents The *NMS* 2004, the *NSCT*, February 2003, and the *National Strategy to Combat Weapons of Mass Destruction*, December 2002 all of which include preemption as a strategy for combating terrorism.

Subordinate Question 2: Is there historical precedence for preemptive war? There are literally hundreds of examples of state actions that can be construed as preemptive in character. Five have been specifically chosen because of their relevance to the United States' National Security challenges of today. Each of these case studies examines the reasons behind the intervention and their legality. The 1967 War case study is preemption in its clearest form. State A, Israel, suspecting an imminent attack by state B, Egypt, reacts to the threat by striking the first blow and devastating state B's war making capability. The second case study, the Israeli strike on Osiraq, involves the actions of one state when it believed that it was faced with a clear nuclear threat. The third case study, the 1982 invasion of Lebanon, is an examination of a state conducting antiterrorist operations by invading a third-party country in order to deny the enemy sanctuaries. The final case study is the United States' attack on Iraq in 2002, often used as an example of preemption, and the justification used to legitimize the action. Israeli military history is not the subject of this research, nor is the political circumstances, either international or domestic, necessarily similar. These examples lend themselves to review because they are controversial and set international legal precedents that are relevant to the adoption and execution of the *NSS* policy of preemption.

The Six-Day War

In June 1967, the Government of Israel believed that the surrounding Arab nations were preparing launch an attack to destroy their state. Constant anti-Zionist rhetoric combined with the withdrawal, requested by Nasser, of United Nations peacekeepers from the Sinai Peninsula, led the Prime Minster to decide to attack first. Israel Air Force planes struck Egyptian air bases first, destroying the bulk of the Egyptian Air Force on the ground and then turned against Jordan and Syria. At the behest of the United Nations Security Council, a cease-fire was arranged but there no peace treaties signed until the first one between Israel and Egypt in 1979 and Israel and Jordan in 1994. The war between Israel and Syria continues (Dinstein 2001, 53). The Israeli action in

26

1967 is regarded as a clear example of a preemptive attack. A state, threatened with imminent attack, struck its enemies first.

Michael Oren in *Six Days of War* attempts to present an unbiased and "balanced study of the military and political facets of the war" (2003, xiv). The political aspect is particularly important because of the spectacular military events, most authors "focused on the military phase of the war" (2003, xiii). The decision to go to war is by definition a political one and Oren traces the political decisions made by key leaders on all sides, which brought about the war and demonstrates an almost inevitable buildup to war. These decision-makers include Soviet, American, and United Nations officials.

Balanced views are important for historians, but they sometimes do not accurately reflect the feelings of the participants at the time of the action. This is particularly important to the concept of imminence or immediacy, which may be more subjective than objective. Chaim Herzog, an Israeli Major General, in *The War of Atonement, October 1973*, as a preamble lays out the Israeli view of the imminence of the Arab threat in 1967. His point of view is included for this reason that the Israelis believed themselves under threat of imminent attack and could under international law defend themselves.

Trevor N. Dupuy in *Elusive Victory: The Arab-Israeli Wars, 1947-1974* expresses the opposite view, that "neither Nasser, nor any other responsible Arab leader wanted war to break out at this time" (Dupuy 1984, 224), therefore the Israeli attack met neither the criterion for immediacy nor necessity. Dupuy is one of the authors that Oren says is "focused on the military phase of the war" and implies that Dupuy exercises some bias in his work (Oren 2003, xiii-xiv). To resolve this, the reader must go back to Dinstein in that:

Hindsight knowledge, suggesting that--notwithstanding the well-founded contemporaneous appraisal of events--the situation may have been less desperate than it appeared is immaterial. The invocation of the right of self-defence must be weighed on the ground of the information available (and reasonably interpreted) at the moment of action, without the benefit of post factum wisdom. (2001, 173)

To underline this, is John G. Stoessinger's interpretation of the events leading up to the 1967 War in *Why Nations go to War*. Stoessinger focuses on the decision making of goIng to war, as he puts it the "human essence of the problem" (Stoessinger 2001, xv). He refers, justifiably enough, to the Arab-Israeli war as the "Fifty Years War" because, despite chronological separation, each engagement (such as 1949, 1956, 1967, and 1982) can only be understood within the context of the whole. Stoessinger includes an excerpt written by an Egyptian Journalist prior to the attack, evaluating Israel's strategic situation in 1967 and concluding, "that Israel must attack" (Stoessinger 2001, 160).

The Israeli Strike on Osiraq

In 1981, Iraq with technical assistance provided by France was close to completing a nuclear power generation plant that would also produce weapons grade uranium. Iraq, even in the midst of war with Iran, repeatedly stated that any weapons produced would not be used against Arabs but against the Israel. Faced with a potentially nuclear holocaust, the government of Menachem Begin was determined to prevent the plant from going into operations. Israeli Air Force pilots were trained and provided with the newest American aircraft to conduct the strike. The strike was executed prior to the plant's going on-line to avoid nuclear collateral damage. The question of imminence and proportionality is important in this case. The Israeli's determined that if the plant went into operation any strike would have unpredictable consequences. Their view of Michael Schmitt's window of opportunity ended when the plant became operational. The choice of time and means to conduct the strike limited significantly the collateral damage and suggests Webster's concept of proportionality. Few casualties were caused by the strike itself, although Saddam Hussein meted out justice to the Iraqi Air Defense units that failed to protect the site.

The Israeli strike on the Iraqi nuclear reactor at the Al Tuwaitha Nuclear Center, Osiraq, in 1981 was conducted in the belief that the Iraqis would use it to build nuclear weapons to use against Israel and therefore met the requirements of necessity and immediacy. Rodger W Claire's *Raid on the Sun* details the political and military preparations for the attack. Most interesting is the presentation of the deep divide within the Israeli cabinet on whether to take the action. While sympathetic towards the pilots, the work is fairly unbiased in rendering the picture of the political situation and struggle prior to the raid. Particularly interesting is the interpretation and weight of statements made by United States politicians in the Israeli Cabinet's decision making process.

The Federation of American Scientists web site has a detailed description of the Osiraq nuclear program and the Israeli strike that destroyed the reactor. The article presents arguments made in support of and against the requirement for the raid. It also adds that the nuclear fuel remained and the Iraqis attempted to build a bomb just prior to the first Gulf War in 1990.

The Jewish Virtual Library maintains a short article entitled "Raid on the Iraqi Reactor." Almost devoid of information, it nevertheless quotes the Israel Defense Forces, Chief of Staff, Lieutenant General Rafel Eitan, in regards to the aid that "The alternative is our destruction."

Professor Louis Beres and Colonel, Israeli Defense Forces (IDF), Yoash Tsiddon-Chatto, in their article "In Support of Anticipatory Self-Defense: Israel, Osiraq, and International Law" contend that anticipatory self-defense is a "long standing customary right." This is a debatable statement in terms of international law, whether it meets the criteria of necessity, proportionality, and immediacy. In the very next paragraph, they claim that a state of war existed between Iraq and Israel to preclude claims of Israeli aggression. This leads to an argumentative conundrum, if Israel and Iraq were already at war, why claim anticipatory self-defense?

The 1982 Israeli Invasion of Lebanon

The Israeli invasion of Lebanon in 1982 was an attempt to deny sanctuary to terrorists in planning, preparing, and launching attacks. In conducting extraterritorial law enforcement by attacking the terrorists within Lebanese sovereignty, Israel was exercising a form of self-defense in which a state "is entitled to enforce international law extra-territorially only when [a second state, in this case Lebanon] is unable or unwilling to prevent repetition of that armed attack" (Dinstein 2003, 217). The Israelis asserted that it was necessary to prevent and preempt further attacks by guerrillas into northern Israel. Kicked out of Jordan by King Hussein, the Palestinian Liberation Organization (PLO) and competing factions began operating out of Southern Lebanon. The Lebanese Government had essentially lost control of its own territory and could not prevent the raid from being launched. Flush with the success of the Osiraq raid, the government of Menachem Begin was determined to clear the terrorists out of Southern Lebanon and protect settlers in Northern Israel. What resulted was a bloody war of attrition, whose political repercussions fractured the Jewish state itself and dragged the United States,

30

among others, militarily into the conflict. That Israel had a right to do for Lebanon what it could not or would not do for it-self in attacking the terrorist enclaves is supported by the Corfu Case and John Quincy Adams retort to Spain in 1818. Israel failed to respond to the terrorist attacks proportionately. Instead, they attacked all the way to Beirut, risking war with Syria and in contradiction to promises made by Menachem Begin to the President of the United States. Israel's disproportionate attack resulted in a quagmire that eventually prompted United States involvement in the peacekeeping operations in Beirut that resulted in the terrorist murder of over 243 United States Marines.

Many of the works that touched on the Six Day War and the raid on Osiraq are also relevant to discussions on the 1982 invasion of Lebanon. Oren asserts that Menachem Begin and Ariel Sharon, taking advantage of their successful strike on Osiraq, took the opportunity to clear the PLO out of Lebanon (Oren 2003, 232). Dinstein approaches it from a legal angle, citing the Corfu Channel case of 1949 "that every state is under an obligation 'not to allow knowingly its territory to be used for acts contrary to the rights of other states'" (Dinstein 2001, 214). Christine Gray in *International Law and the Use of Force*, points out that Israel had been supplying weapons to Christian factions in Lebanon as a counterbalance to Syria's stationing of troops in Lebanon at the invitation of the Lebanese President (Gray 2000, 73). This work examines the use of force in international relations and the impact of regional and supra-regional organizations involved in collective security.

<u>The United States Invasion of Iraq, 2003</u>

<u>Subordinate Question 3: Was the United States attack on Iraq in 2003 an example of a preemptive strategy?</u> In *The Iraq War*, John Keegan depicts the United States

invasion of Iraq in 2003. Published in 2004, almost immediately after the events described, the work is limited to only the defeat of Saddam and the fall of his regime. Ironically it begins, "Some wars begin badly. Some end badly. The Iraq War of 2003 was exceptional in both beginning well for the Anglo-American force that waged it and ending victoriously" (Keegan 2004, 1). One wonders if he has begun revising for a second edition yet. However even a military historian of unquestioned credibility, such as Keegan seems unsure of the definition of preemption, defining it as "striking first to avert a later danger" (Keegan 2004, 95). This clearly is at odds with Nye's definition of preemption, "A preemptive strike occurs when war is imminent" and more in line with his definition of preventive war which "occurs when statesmen believe merely that war is better now than later" (2003, 157). Not really a surprising or difficult mistake to make considering that President Bush and his administration of neo-conservatives used the words preemption and prevention interchangeably, and confusingly, in the *NSS* of 2002.

For legal discussion on the United States invasion of Iraq, this research will once again look to Michael Schmitt. First, "International Law and the Use of Force: Attacking Iraq" in the February 2003 edition of the *Royal United Services Institute Journal*. Next, "The Legality of Operation Iraqi Freedom under International Law," published in the *Journal of Military Ethics* in 2004. In both articles, Schmitt advances that Iraq's material breach of the 1991 cease-fire terms was a stronger basis for war than either WMD or the terrorism connection.

However, interviews conducted by Anthony Dworkin for "Iraq and the Bush Doctrine of Preemptive Self Defense" state that the United Nations resolution establishing the cease-fire "did not make the ceasefire conditional on Iraq's future cooperation with inspections" and believes that convincing evidence of WMD production would have more relevance to getting international approval, in the form of a new resolution, for a resumption of hostilities. Schmitt's argument is "that the Security Council itself has repeatedly found Iraq in material breach of the cease-fire terms" (Schmitt 2003, 15).

Summary

There is an abundance of official and unofficial material relating to the history, policy, legality, and execution of preemptive war available. However, central to this current controversy is the publication of the *NSS* of 2002 that adopts pre-emption as an official government policy of the United States. Clearly, its current legality is in question, but as Dinstein points out the common practice of states over time can become customary international law. There is a definition and precedence set for the conduct of preemptive strikes. The adoption by the United States of a policy of preemption sets an international standard that, despite a seemingly hypocritical stance by the United States discouraging its use by other nations, implicitly allows other nations to act in the same manner. The challenge lies in the motives of these other nations, and many would say the United States, in taking preemptive action. Motives may not always be so pure.

CHAPTER 3

RESEARCH METHODOLOGY

> The line it is drawn
> The curse it is cast
> The slow one now
> Will later be fast
> As the present now
> Will later be past
> The order is
> Rapidly fadin'.
> And the first one now
> Will later be last
> For the times they are a-changin'.
>
> Bob Dylan, *The Times They Are A-Changin*

Introduction

The times were changing; the question was how? The fall of the Soviet Union fundamentally changed the strategic paradigm that had existed since the end of World War II and the beginning of the Cold War. The polarized international system that existed previously, and kept the world relatively stable, was now like a man with a broken leg and only one crutch. The other crutch having been unexpectedly and violently torn away, he now hobbles in search of equilibrium lost.

United States Strategy: Cold War

During the cold war, there were two independent variables, the means and the ends. The means were the conventional forces, interagency cooperation, and the elements of national power Diplomatic, Information, Military, and Economic. The ends were the security of the state. The dependent variable was the ways, which meant large conventional and nuclear forces supporting a strategy of deterrence, or mutual assured destruction. "In the Cold War, especially after the Cuban missile crisis, we faced a generally status quo, risk adverse adversary. Deterrence was an effective defense" (*NSS* 2002, 15). Deterrence and containment were the predominant strategies used in the Cold War because there were two main antagonists with their supporting alliances, generally thought to be equally matched in terms of diplomatic, economic, and military strength. The international political system remained stable and wars were, for the most part, kept short and small by international intervention in order to reduce the chances that they would expand into a super power conflict with the attendant dangers of escalation to nuclear one.

Terror was a relatively small-scale strategy, if highly electrifying, used by elements that could not engage in conventional great power warfare or as a form of proxy war between the two superpowers. It was a crime to be investigated, perpetrators arrested, and adjudicated by the judicial systems of affected countries. Terrorism was a tactic often used by proxy and supported by large nations to achieve their goals but not risk a war that might not be controllable once unleashed. The conditions over which this all played out, was that of a bi-polar world, kept in check by the two dominant super powers. With sizable numbers of nuclear weapons available, the stakes of letting the cold war turn hot, even for brushfire wars, were too high to risk without at least tacit acceptance of that strategy by both powers. See figure 1.

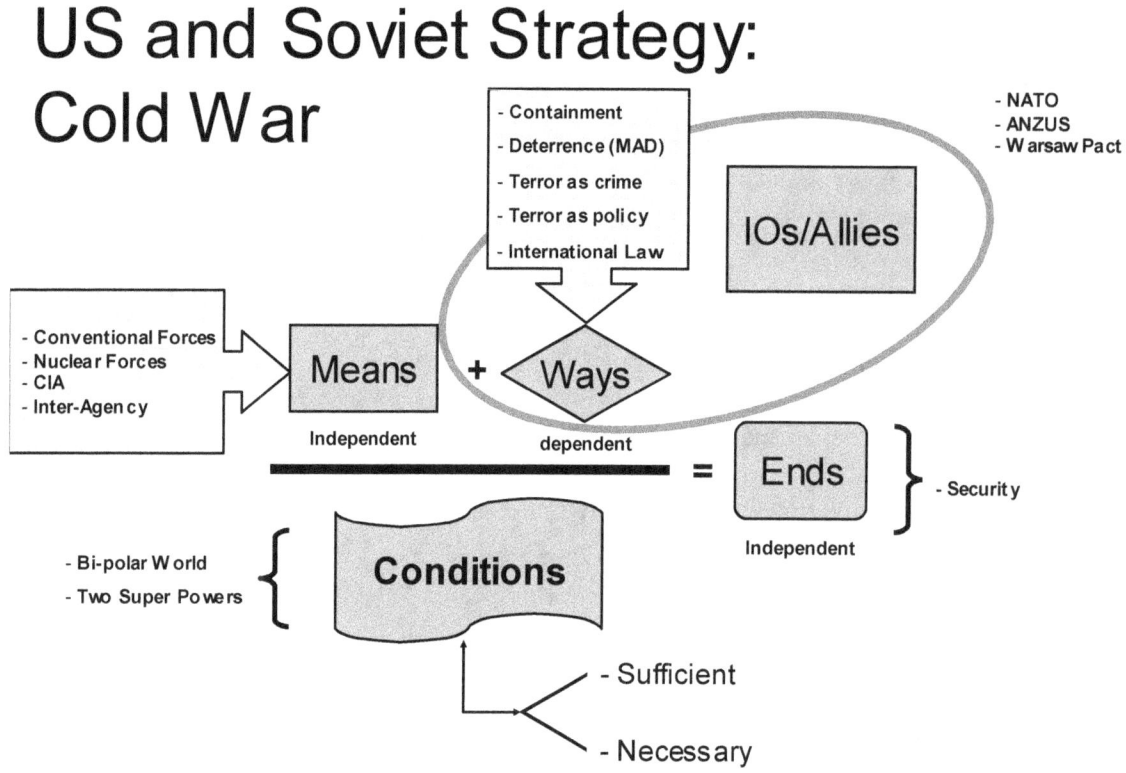

Figure 1.   United States and Soviet Strategy, Cold War

<u>United States Strategy: Post-Cold War - Pre 11 September</u>

When the Soviet Union fell so dramatically, the United States' perception of the

system remained relatively unchanged, except that there was now only one super power.

The independent variables of means and ends remained the same, as did the ways or the

dependent variable. The only major shift in perception was the diminishing of nuclear

weapons as a factor in deterrence. The Russians were destroying large portions of their

arsenal and the threat to national security had devolved on to the regional stage with

regional powers affecting national interests in those regions and not national security of

the United States as a whole. In fact, many thought war as a state practice was on the decline as indicated by the comments of the United Nations Secretary General in 1995: "At the time, there was a widespread belief that when no longer fuelled by rival major powers the many regional conflicts flaring in different parts of the world would quickly be extinguished" (Gray 2000, 1).

At the same time many of treaties that bound nations together evaporated, as in the case of the Warsaw Pact, or "loosened" of their own accord when the pressure of a second belligerent super power was released. Two prominent examples are the Warsaw Pact and the ANZUS Treaty. The Australian-New Zealand-United States Treaty (ANZUS) "loosened" towards the end of the cold war when the United States "suspended its ANZUS security obligations" with New Zealand over that nation's refusal to allow nuclear powered and nuclear armed ship visits (U.S. Department of State 2004, 6).

This is reflected in the Clinton Administration's policy of "Enlargement and Engagement" as readily perceived in their December 1999, National Security Strategy document, *A National Security Strategy for a Global Age*. Like national security strategies published before, it reflected more of what the Clinton Administration was already doing rather than presenting a vision from which to build policy, reading more like a resume than a policy statement (Gaddis 2004a, 65). However, the document clearly reflects the belief that terrorism is a crime, "When terrorism occurs . . . we can neither forget the crime nor ever give up on bringing its perpetrators to justice" (*NSS* 2000, 22). As a crime, therefore it will be handled as a criminal matter by police agencies, "Since 1993, the FBI's counterterrorism budget and the number of FBI agents assigned to counterterrorism have more than doubled" (*NSS* 2000, 23). And, in fact, a military option was at the bottom of available courses of action and only in response to a terrorist incident and the failure of other agencies to achieve results. "Our strategy pressures terrorists, deters attacks, and responds forcefully to terrorist acts. It combines enhanced law enforcement and intelligence efforts; vigorous diplomacy and economic sanctions; and, when necessary, military force" (*NSS* 2000, 22).

Integral to the Clinton Administration's policy of anti-terrorism was the concept of deterrence. The concept, a holdover from the Cold War, anticipated that terrorists would be deterred by the overwhelming strength of the United States and established force protection measures. In short, the terrorists would be dissuaded from terrorist action by the difficulty of striking American targets and the punishment that would inevitably follow. "Whether at home or abroad, we will respond to terrorism through defensive readiness of our facilities and personnel and the ability of our terrorism consequence management efforts to mitigate injury and damage" (*NSS* 2000, 22). What was not really comprehended was that the terrorists would then seek targets that were not as protected.

The Clinton policy was in essence a defensive policy, focused on preventing terrorist attacks though diplomatic and legal means, only considering the military option to respond after the incident occurred. See figure 2.

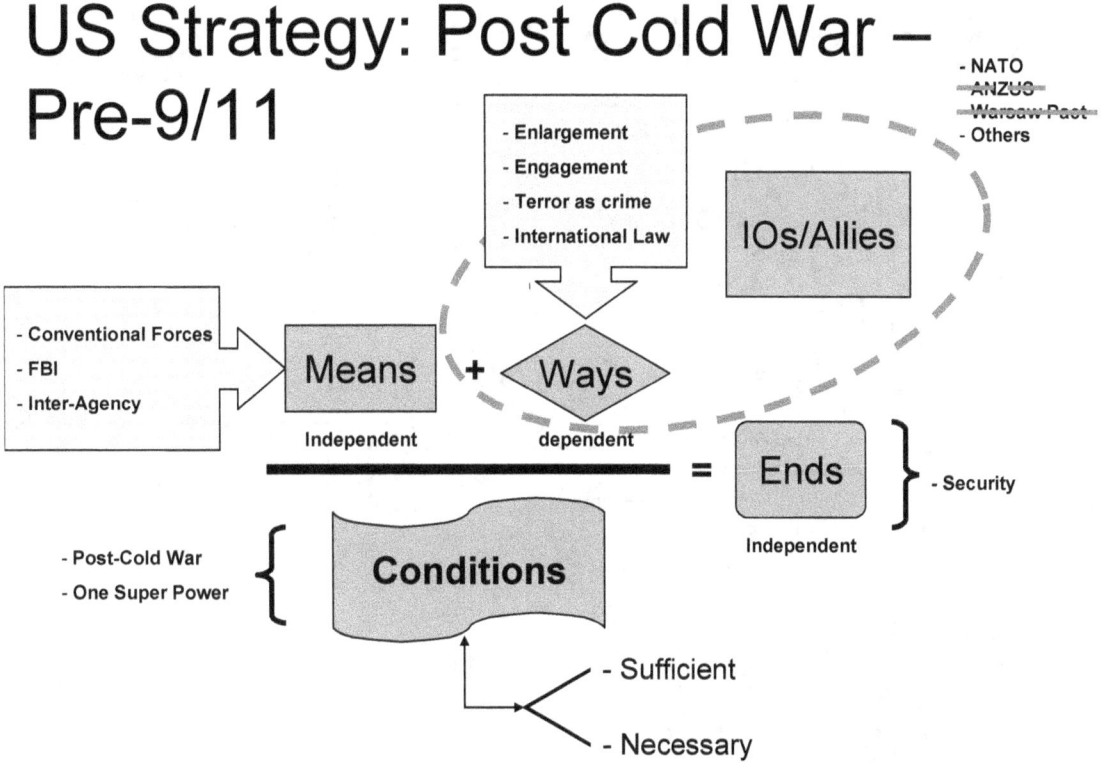

Figure 2.   United States Strategy, Post-Cold War-Pre 11 September

<u>United States Strategy: Post-11 September</u>

When the conditions changed however, for example, two superpowers to one, the

whole international system also changed, "distant disputes became less relevant to the

balance of power" (Nye 2003, 189). International organizations, while important before,

assumed a new significance. International organizations that were kept in line by the

nature of the bi-polar world continued to be less responsive to U.S. pressure, such as

NATO's failure to participate in the invasion of Iraq despite their support for the United

States in Afghanistan. See figure 3.

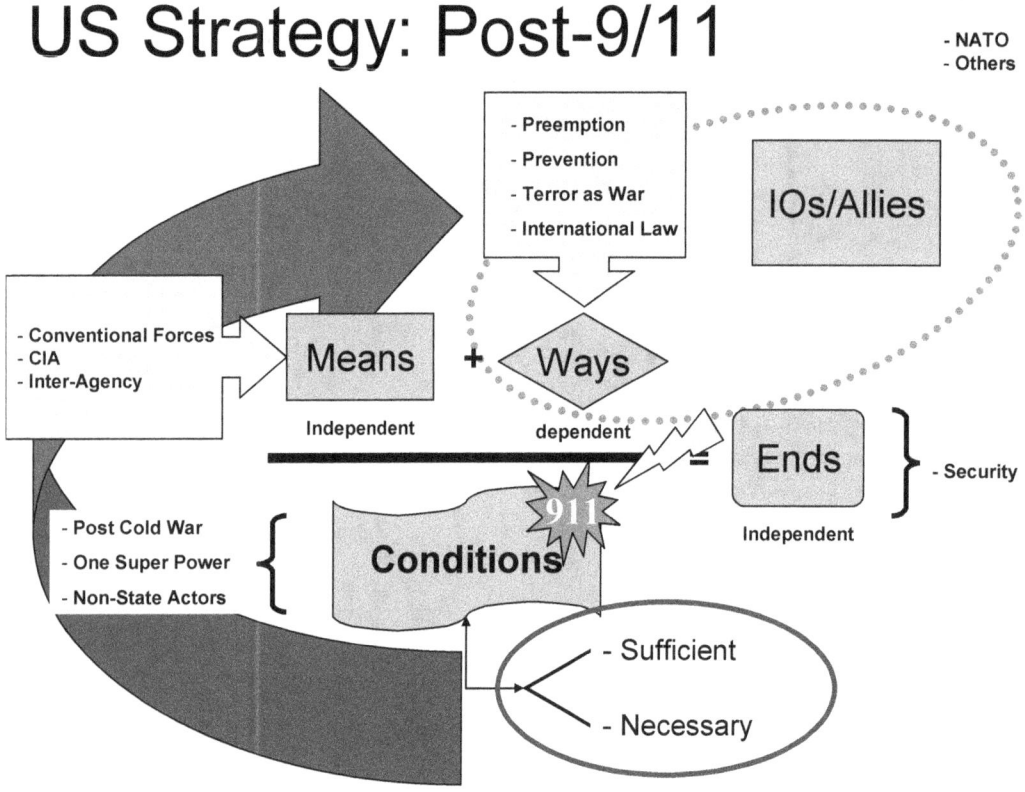

Figure 3.   United States Strategy, Post-11 September

The loosening of the bipolar international system that existed during the Cold War enabled the rise of non-state actors to prominence and power in pursuit of their own, vice superpower, agendas. Non-state actors had always existed and utilized the elements of power: diplomatic, information, military and economic, to achieve their ends. What fundamentally changed was the belated recognition that these transnational non-state actors developed the capability to organize and commit large-scale attacks such as the strikes on the World Trade Center, the Pentagon, and rail system in Madrid. This, coupled with the availability of nuclear, chemical, and biological research and materials since the end of the cold war, caused a fundamental shift in how the administration viewed national security strategy. The threat of terrorists or rogue states achieving relative nuclear parity was too great, and potentially too devastating, to continue with deterrence and a legal methodology to attack terrorism.

The Bush Administration pointed out the failure to comprehend the new strategic environment, or conditions under which strategy was developed, in the *NSS* of 2002. "It has taken almost a decade for us to comprehend the true nature of this new threat. Given the goals of rogue states and terrorists, the United States can no longer solely rely on a reactive posture as we have in the past" (*NSS* 2002, 15).

The events of 11 September, while indicating the failure of legal means of prevention, also indicated the failure of deterrence to prevent terrorist attacks. "Traditional concepts of deterrence will not work against an enemy whose avowed tactics are wanton destruction and the targeting of innocents; whose so-called soldiers seek martyrdom in death and whose most potent protection is statelessness" (*NSS* 2002, 15). Deterrence, that strategic staple of the Cold War and holdover in the years between the fall of the Soviet Union and 11 September 2001, was shown to be irrelevant as an anti-terror strategy when the passenger aircraft crashed into the World Trade Center and the Pentagon. The Bush administration was left with the question of how to prevent this from occurring again.

Their answer, also reflected in the *NSS* of 2002, was a policy of preemption against rogue states and terrorist in order to deny them the opportunity to inflict another 11 September, or an even more disastrous incident involving some form of WMD, on the United States. With the adoption of the *NSS* of 2002, the Bush Administration formally announced to the world that preemption, while not the only policy, was never the less an integral part of the national security strategy.

Preemption, as discussed in chapter one, is a legal act, provided it meets the criteria established by Daniel Webster in the Caroline Case of necessity, proportionality, and imminence (or immediacy) (Walzer 2000, 74). Within the context of the dangers of WMD, the Bush Administration directly addresses the concept of immediacy in terms of "today's threats" in its *NSS* (2002, 15). Ergo, the United States would be entirely within its rights to act preemptively provided it meets the above criteria. However, that is not necessarily the way the international system works. It is an increasingly interdependent system, where the action of one state, regardless of its size or reckoned power, affects other states. Nye writes, "system effects--where small perturbations in one can spread throughout a whole system--become more important" (Nye 2003, 189). Therefore any execution of the strategy of preemption must result from conditions, sufficient and necessary, that will be acceptable to the international community, defined in this thesis as the five permanent members of the United Nations Security Council. It is these sufficient and necessary conditions that drive United States strategy. No longer, as in the cold war, can the United States act with expected (read unquestioned?) acquiescence of its policies even from allies. However, it also does not mean that the United States, or any nation, is prevented from acting in the face of an imminent threat. The question of "sufficient" and "necessary" conditions will be explored by using the following set of criteria on preemption to evaluate the three Israeli case studies in table 1.

Table 1.   Israeli Case Study Analysis

Conflict	NSS Applicability	Imminence of Attack		No Viable Alternatives	Proportionality	Legitimacy
		Immediacy	Schmitt's "Last Window of Opportunity"			
1967 Arab-Israeli War	Conventional Warfare					
Osirak Raid (Israel vs. Iraq)	WMD					
1982 Israeli invasion of Lebanon	Terrorism					

Self Defense – "Caroline Case" Webster

  Conditions for Criteria Met

  Conditions for Criteria Partially Met

As each case study is evaluated, and the criterion is judged to have been met, an explosion mark will be placed in the criteria box corresponding to that case study. If the criterion is judged as having been partially met an outlined explosion mark will be placed in the criteria box corresponding to that case study. If the criterion is judged not to have been met at all, the criteria box corresponding to that case study will remain empty. Once an understanding of the criteria is established by analyzing the Israeli experience with preemptive and preventive attacks. The same criteria will be applied to conflicts the United States has engaged in or is facing as articulated in table 2.

Table 2.   United States Case Study Analysis

Conflict	NSS Applicability	Imminence of Attack		No Viable Alternatives	Proportionality	Legitimacy
		Immediacy	Schmitt's "Last Window of Opportunity"			
2003 US invasion of Iraq	Conventional Warfare					
North Korea	Nexus of WMD and Terrorism					
Iran	Terrorism					

Self Defense – "Caroline Case" Webster

  Conditions for Criteria Met

  Conditions for Criteria Partially Met

Each of the conflicts was chosen because of the applicability to the *NSS* of 2002, specifically the twin threats of terrorism and WMD. The determination of whether a conflict is unresolved or resolved, relates to the environment that existed, or causal factors, when a preemptive action was taken. A discussion of the criterion selected and the international legal basis for preemption, or anticipatory self-defense, follows.

Self-Defense: The Caroline Case

As noted in the graph, the criteria of necessity, proportionality, and imminence are derived directly from Daniel Webster's protest against British violation of American sovereignty in the Caroline Case in 1842. That in order to legitimately conduct an act of anticipatory self-defense, a state must be able to demonstrate the "necessity of self-defence, instant, over-whelming, leaving no choice of means, and no moment for deliberation and the acts could not be unreasonable or excessive" (Schmitt 2003b, 530).

Imminence

The criterion of imminence is the requirement of instant action "leaving no moment for deliberation" (Schmitt 2003b, 533). It must be shown that the requirement to take action was precipitated by an impending threat from an aggressor nation. An offended nation need not wait until it is attacked, with all of the consequent destruction, to respond "with the perception of urgency" to the threat (Dinstein 2001, 219). Significantly, Dinstein also states that, "The invocation of the right of self-defence must be weighed on the ground of information available [and reasonable interpreted] at the moment of action, without the benefit of *post factum* wisdom" (Dinstein 2001, 173). This means that the offended nation must be judged on the evidence they possessed at the time of decision and not based on information discovered or revealed at a later time.

Last Window of Opportunity

The last window of opportunity as a condition of preemptive strike is derived from Michael N. Schmitt and is directly related to the question of imminence as defined by terrorism and WMD. In other words, the circumstances of a terrorist attack may not allow interception of the action when it is imminent. The nature of terrorism may only allow the threatened nation one window of opportunity prior to the strike and that may be months prior to the execution date. If this is acceptable, then the criterion of imminence changes fundamentally when referring to a terror attack or a conventional attack.

No Viable Alternatives

The criterion of "viable alternatives" is based on Webster's standard of necessity, "leaving no choice of means" and "no moment for deliberation" (McCoubrey and White 1992, 92), in "that all reasonable alternatives to the use of force be exhausted" (Schmitt 2003b, 530). In that "If a State wishes to act preemptively, then it must be certain beyond reasonable doubt that either the Security Council will fail to act or that any action it might take will be unsuccessful in deterring the threat" (Schmitt 2003b, 531).

In short, that the offended state had no other recourse but to act in the manner chosen with the tools at hand to preempt and attack. Either all avenues must be exhausted prior to the action and the United Nations failed to act or their efforts were not successful.

Proportionality

The final criterion specified by Webster, and accepted by both the Nuremberg Tribunal and the International Court of Justice, is proportionality, in that an attack in response to an imminent threat may not be "unreasonable or excessive" (Schmitt 2003b, 530). In short, the amount force used must be justified by the level of the threat and may not do more damage than is necessary to remove said threat.

Legitimacy

The final condition to set the stage for a preemptive action must be legitimacy. What constitutes legitimacy, and how is it derived, for an act that seemingly violates the established Westphalian order of the supremacy of the state system in international affairs? For the United States, at least, legitimacy begins with the people and the consent

of the governed. This is clearly seen in the preamble to the Declaration of Independence,

> We hold these truths to be self-evident, that all men are created equal, that they are endowed by their Creator with certain unalienable rights, that among these are Life, Liberty and the pursuit of Happiness. That to secure these rights, *Governments are instituted by Men, deriving their just Powers from the consent of the governed,* (Emphasis mine) That whenever any Form of Government becomes destructive of these ends, it is the Right of the People to alter or abolish it, and to institute new Government.

It is this same spirit that animated the United States in its leadership of the free world

during the Cold War, by seeking to "apply the practices of domestic democratic statecraft

internationally" (Gaddis 2004b, 64). This in effect meant that NATO, particularly, and

the United Nations, generally, were representative bodies whose members, not unlike the

"Men" referred to in the passage above, had their own beliefs and special circumstances

that dictated their own distinct national interests. This consideration of the opinions of

others is also indicated in the Declaration of Independence, "a *decent respect to the*

opinions of mankind [emphasis mine] requires that they should declare the causes which

impel them to the separation." This demonstrates the integral belief in a community of

nations even at the dawn of American history. As a result the United States throughout

the Cold War had to demonstrate as much a moral as political leadership in international

relations. This is in direct contrast to the Soviet ideological claim to moral superiority and

leadership that was undercut by their own actions and coercive policies towards allies,

such as the Warsaw Pact, resulting directly in the eventual dissolution of the Soviet

Union as a State (Gaddis 2004b, 78). This requirement for leadership, instead of

diminishing in the absence of an "Evil Empire," has burgeoned along with the

responsibility and perceptions in the international community. One need only look to the

47

protestations in the aftermath of the great tsunami the struck in late 2004, where are the Americans? Why are they not reacting quickly enough? And when the United States did react, why they were not donating more? Some of these pointed questions were directed from nations that openly criticized America's intervention in Iraq. If the United States still must exhibit moral as well as political leadership in the age of one superpower, then the measure of that leadership is the ability to influence nations positively, or at least not negatively, towards their policies. An indicator, therefore, to the effectiveness of the leadership of the United States is the reaction of the international community as reflected in the voting records (specifically whether a veto occurred) of the five permanent members of the United Nations Security Council: the United States, the United Kingdom, Russia, the Peoples' Republic of China, and France. These five nations represent widely disparate internal governmental systems whose power has brought them to the pinnacle of the international community, as judged by the status as permanent members of the United Nations Security Council and the veto power that accompanies this status. Buttressing their status, aside from the veto power, is the authority conferred on the United Nations Security Council by Article 51 of the United Nations Charter to take "measures necessary to maintain international peace and security" (Gray 2000, 88). In effect, the Security Council as an international body representing the people of the world has the authority to declare war and mobilize sufficient resources through the constituent states to conduct war. A constant reminder is the existence of the United Nations Command in South Korea, relic of a war voted for and resourced by the United Nations in 1950 and continuing to this day. The backing of the world as a result, through this international body, constitutes legitimacy in and of itself. However, this also means that

48

these states will be the ones most impacted by Nye's "small perturbations" (Nye 2003, 189). Therefore, it is their acceptance or acquiescence, after the fact, of an action that determines legitimacy. This is reflected in the resolutions considered and adopted by the United Nations Security Council regarding that same action.

Conclusion

The United States must set the conditions for the legitimacy of any preemptive act prior to the actual conduct of said act. To do this, the United States must start by complying with the principles of imminence, proportionality, and necessity as established by Daniel Webster in the Caroline Case. Most importantly, the United States must have the backing of the international community. After the disaster of 11 September 2001, the United States arguably had been granted the latitude by the international community to conduct preemptive strikes as indicated by the resolutions condemning terrorism subsequently passed by the United Nations Security Council. In the GWOT, the United States must proactively shape the battlefield and that claiming to lead the war on terror, or "coalitions of the willing," does not necessarily meet the requirement. It requires positively influencing nations to agree, acquiesce, to the policies and actions of the United States. This does not mean that the five permanent members of the Security Council have a say in how the United States reacts to terrorism in the aftermath of 11 September, but that any act of preemption by the United States must take place in an atmosphere created to induce approval by those member states. In short, sustained moral and political leadership by the United States will build the legitimacy required as the "sufficient and necessary" preparatory condition to conduct preemptive action. This legitimacy will be reflected in the reactions of the five permanent members of the United Nations Security Council.

CHAPTER 4

ANALYSIS

The nation exists before everything; it is at the origin of
everything; its will is always legal, it is the law itself.

Knox and Murray,
The Dynamics of Military Revolution, 1300-2050

Inter arma silent leges [in time of war, the laws are silent]

Walzer, *Just and Unjust Wars*

Introduction

The following case studies will examine the sufficient and necessary conditions

that caused the Israeli Government to take preemptive action. Each case study has a

direct relationship to the threats that the United States faces today as addressed in the *NSS*

of 2002. The 1967 War case study looks at a preemptive strike against a conventional

threat or peer competitor in terms of the national security strategy. The second case study,

the Israeli Air Forces raid on Osirak in 1981, evaluates the shaping of the international

environment and the consequences of a preemptive military strike against the threat of

WMD, in this case the development of nuclear weapons by Iraq. The third case study is

an assessment of the 1982 Israeli invasion of Lebanon to remove a terrorist threat, also

with particular emphasis on the shaping of the international environment and the effect of

that effort on the determination of the legitimacy of the strike in the international

community. As each case study is evaluated, marks will be placed in the case study chart

to assist in identifying those sufficient and necessary conditions that need to exist to

ensure the international legitimacy of a preemptive action and the subsequent reaction of

the international community.

51

1967 Arab-Israeli War

Background

Just after dawn on the morning of 5 June 1967, three waves of forty aircraft each

launched from Israeli Air Force Bases and flew west into the Mediterranean in

accordance with a pattern set since 1965 (Dupuy 1984, 243). Instead of returning to their

bases as usual, the aircraft turned south, crossed into Egyptian sovereign territory, and

struck multiple Egyptian Air Force airfields. In all they destroyed 300 aircraft on the

ground and shot down the eight MiG-21s that managed to get airborne (Dupuy 1984,

246). Thus with a preemptive or surprise attack, Israel began the third Arab-Israeli War.

In early May, the Soviets reported an Israeli military buildup aimed at Syria (Oren

2003, 55). Despite reports from one of their own generals and the Chief United Nations

observer Odd Bull, that they saw no Israeli buildup in the Golan Heights area, Egyptian

forces were peremptorily ordered into the Sinai. On 17 May, Egyptian jets approaching

from Jordanian air space conducted a reconnaissance of the Israeli nuclear facility at

Dimona (see figure 4) (Oren 2003, 75). On 18 May, Egypt formally requested the United

Nations to withdraw the United Nations Emergency Force (UNEF), a peacekeeping force

established after the 1956 Arab-Israeli War to act as a buffer between Israel and Egypt,

from the Sinai Peninsula. The Secretary General, without recourse to the General

Assembly or Security Council, complied with the Egyptian demand by authorizing the

withdrawal of UNEF in its entirety (Oren 2003, 73). Not waiting for formal withdrawal

of UNEF, however, Egyptian forces circumvented the peacekeepers and assumed

positions along the border with Israel (Oren 2003, 70). By 19 May, there were six full

Egyptian Divisions in the Sinai (Oren 2003, 78), including the 4th Armored Division,

Nasser's "best" which to the Israeli's deemed to be "indications and warning" (Oren

2003, 62-63). See figure 4.

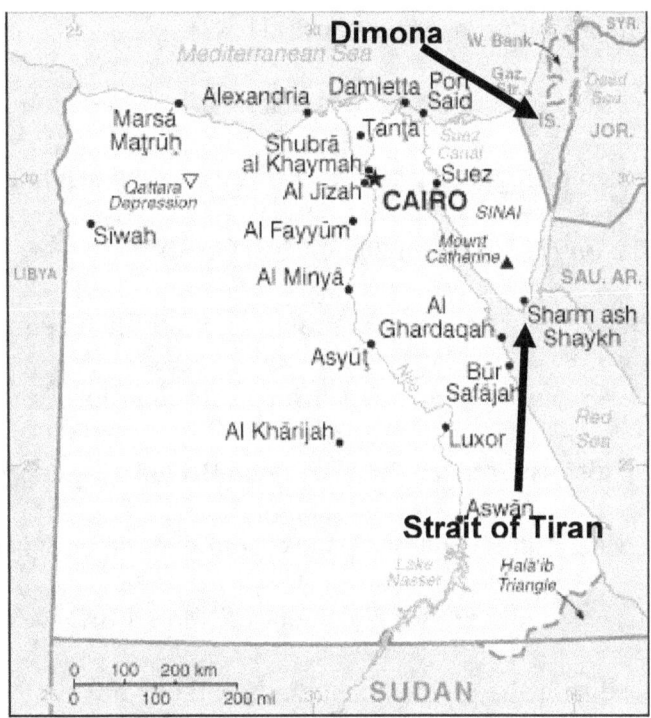

Figure 4.   Egypt and the Sinai

Source: CIA, *Fact Book*, 2005, available from http://www.cia.gov/cia/publications/
factbook/geos/eg.html; Internet; accessed on 10 May 2005.

On 22 May, Nasser ordered the Strait of Tiran closed to Israeli flagged shipping

despite the agreements made in 1956 to respect the free use of the waterway. In effect

establishing a blockade and committing an act of aggression as defined by the Article 3

of the United Nations General Assembly's Definition of Aggression (Dinstein 2003,

117). At the time of the 1956 agreement, Israel had been guaranteed that "the U.S. would

regard any attempt by Egypt to revive the Tiran blockade as an act of war to which Israel

could respond in self-defense under Article 51 of the UN Charter," provided that the

Israelis informed the United States of their intentions (Oren 2003, 12). Moshe Dayan had included "Freedom of shipping for Israeli vessels in the Gulf of Aqaba," as one of the objectives of the 1956 war (Dupuy 1984, 230). In fact, closure of the Tiran Strait was a significant blow to the Israeli economy (Oren 2003, 83).

Concurrently, the Egyptian Army was planning for Operation Dawn, a surprise attack on Israel. Planned to begin on 28 May, it was cancelled just hours before execution due to Soviet pressure on Nasser (Oren 2003, 120). On 30 May, King Hussein of Jordan signed a mutual-defense treaty with Nasser providing for unified command and control and allowing other Arab nations to move their forces through Jordan to attack Israel (Oren 2003, 130). He also ordered the 40th Armored Brigade, equipped with 100 modern United States-made M48 Patton main battle tanks sold with the proviso that they would be used only for defense, to join the Jordanian 60th Armored Brigade already deployed on the West Bank. The strategic problem that the Israeli Government faced even before the war was immense; a small nation surrounded by well-armed, hostile neighbors,

> All of Israel's major population and industrial centers were within easy artillery range of one or another Arab army. At its narrowest point the country was mere 9 miles wide, easily bifurcated by a Jordanian or and Iraqi thrust from the East, with nowhere to fall back to but the sea. (Oren 2003, 6)

On 4 June, the Commander of the UNEF was in Cairo and read the Egyptian Front Commander's order to his troops to, "reconquer the stolen land . . . with your arms and your united faith . . . the eyes of the world are on you in your glorious war against Israeli aggression" (Oren 2003, 166). Upon returning to his command post in the Sinai, he reported to New York what he had observed during his flight, "Large-scale deployment of UAR army, including tanks and artillery, cannot be for anything but an

54

offensive. There is no suitable defensible position between these points. Implications of Mortaga's [sic] message are evident" (Oren 2003, 167).

Imminence

By 4 June 1967, the Arab states had the equivalent of thirteen Divisions mobilized for war, including modern United States and Soviet made main battle tanks, the M48 Patton and the T-55, with a fourteenth (Iraqi armored) division within striking distance. Jordanian forces were also now integrated into the Arab unified command structure and its two most modern units were deployed on the West Bank. Against the Arab strength, Israel had the equivalent of seven divisions, three of which were predominantly armored (Dupuy 1984, 338). The Egyptians had requested the removal of the border force and closed the Strait of Tiran. The opening of the Strait of Tiran, as a condition for ending the 1956 War, could only be seen as requirement for maintaining the peace and, if closed, would then be a condition for war (Dupuy 1984, 230).

The United Nations' Commander on the scene also believed that an Egyptian attack on Israel was imminent, based essentially on three factors: (1) the previously ordered removal of UNEF, (2) the physical occupation of border posts by Egyptian and Palestinian soldiers, and (3) the massive deployment of Egyptian ground forces that he saw with his own eyes. The Secretary General also clearly foresaw the consequences when the Egyptians first requested that UNEF merely move away from the border saying, "UNEF cannot be asked to stand aside in order to enable the two sides to resume fighting" (Oren 2003, 70).

On 18 May, the Israeli Chief of Intelligence recommended to the Israeli cabinet that the reserves be activated for war, based on his assessment of Arab dispositions and arrangements. On 19 May, almost three weeks before the beginning of the war, the Israeli

Prime Minister, "warned Deputy Defense Minister Zvi Dinstein. 'There's going to be a

war, I'm telling you, there's going to be a war'" (Oren 2003, 77). In other words, if the

Israeli Prime Minister, based on the information he had at the time, reasonably believed

that an assault by Egypt was imminent, then he had a right, duty even, to take preemptive

action. Finally, a macabre indicator of the Israeli Government's belief that war was

imminent throughout May and into June of 1967 is that "thousands of graves were dug in

military cemeteries" (Walzer 2000, 84).

No Viable Alternatives

Did Israel have no viable alternatives and no moment for deliberation when they

launched their air assault on 5 June 1967? As with all catastrophes, there is a chain of

events that, if interdicted at any one point, might have been averted. The large-scale

deployment of the Arab forces dictated the means necessary for Israel to employ in its

defense. The strategic problem Israel faced at the time, no buffer zone between the

frontline and its vital population and industrial centers, dictated that it strike first or risk a

coordinated attack on three fronts. Diplomatic efforts, however, were opened

immediately in response to the first reports of Egyptian forces crossing into the Sinai "the

State Department, the British Foreign Office--any channel to Nasser, even U Thant--was

utilized in assuring Nasser that Israel had no warlike intentions" (Oren 2003, 62). The

indifferent diplomatic response of the United Nations and the five permanent members,

however, "fearing Afro-Asian unity and the Soviet veto, the Western nations refrained

from taking the issue to either the General Assembly or the Security Council" (Oren

2003, 75). This response significantly reduced the alternatives available to the Israeli government. Lukewarm proposals from the United States about international convoys to break the blockade never received much support and were quickly overtaken by events (Oren 2003, 89).

On 25 May, the Israeli Foreign Minister arrived in Washington, via Paris and London, for consultations. His reception in France, despite a previously close relationship was disappointing; De Gaulle, in his counsel that the Israelis should not be the aggressors, pointedly remarked that "this is 1967" not 1956, underlining a distinct change in policy since the Suez Crisis (Oren 2003, 100). A spokesman later stated, "Israel did not have to shoot first to be labeled the aggressor, but merely send a ship through Tiran" (Oren 2003, 101). The British were more supportive and "committed to reopen the Strait through action 'in or outside of the UN'" (Oren 2003, 101). Despite a warning by the British Prime Minister "that Israel would almost certainly go to war unless its Foreign Minister received concrete commitments to its security," the visit to Washington did not produce the commitment to security that the Israeli cabinet desired. Instead, the Israeli Foreign Minister was blandly informed that, "the President could not guarantee Israel's security without congressional approval, which under the circumstances, he was unlikely to get" (Oren 2003, 108). The Soviets seemed to be actively interested in maintaining the crisis and were the source of reports that the Israelis were preparing for an offensive against Syria. Despite numerous invitations to visit the disputed area in order to disprove the reports, the Soviet Ambassador declined. The Soviet Ambassador's earlier statements to the Director General of Israel's Foreign Ministry, however, seemed ominous, "You will be punished for your alliance with imperialism and you will lose your access to the Red Sea" (Oren 2003, 59). Israel even prevailed upon the Secretary General to take a

57

message directly to the Egyptian Government, "that Israel would act militarily to reopen the Strait, had no impact on the [Egyptian] Foreign Minister" (Oren 2003, 85). In fact, every effort was made by the Israeli government to defuse the crisis. Nasser, however, seemed to thrive on crisis because of the prestige he had gained in the Arab World.

Proportionality

Did Israel use more force than required to remove the Arab threat? By 4 June 1967, the combined armies of Egypt, Jordan, and Syria had thirteen divisions under a single, unified, command structure in positions along their borders. These divisions included some of the most modern military equipment available from both the Soviet Union and the United States. Israeli cities were already in range of some artillery in the north and terrorist attacks had been increasing since May. Egyptian Air Force planes were violating Israeli airspace and conducting reconnaissance of the Nuclear Facility at Dimona. On the night of 4 June, "The 275,000 men, 1100 tanks and 200 planes of the Israeli Defence Forces were ready to embark on the largest offensive in Middle East History" (Oren 2003, 168). Still these forces were only directed at Egypt; however in clear attempt to limit the war, Israel would not attack Jordan or Syria unless they attacked first. The Israelis sent a message to King Hussein through the Commanding Officer of the United Nations Treaty Supervision Organization to this effect (Dupuy 1984, 285), though he regarded the message as more of an Israeli threat than an offer to maintain the peace (Oren 2003, 184). It was only after Jordanian artillery, slow to respond initially, shelled a landing strip in the north, that Israel turned on Jordan (Dupuy 1984, 287). By this time, however, Egyptian commandos previously sent to Jordan, and positioned in the West Bank, had already begun operations (Oren 2003, 185).

58

Legitimacy

In the aftermath of 5 June, the resolutions passed by the Security Council singled out no particular nations for condemnation, concentrating instead on finding cease-fire criteria that would be acceptable to all of the belligerents. Each of the belligerents, however, delayed accepting a cease-fire when it believed it was achieving success (Oren 2003, 251). Despite the delays, within five days of the preemptive Israeli attack and four days since the passage of United Nations Security Council Resolution (UNSCR) 233 calling for an "immediate cease-fire and for a cessation of all military activities in the area," all of the nations agreed to the cease-fire. In the end, Israel accepted the cease-fire but did not accept Arab and Soviet demands to withdraw to the pre-June 5 lines of demarcation (Oren 2003, 325). By this time, the United States had also lost patience with Israel, fearing their relations with the Arab Nations in the Middle East would be irrevocably damaged. Finally, on 22 November 1967, UNSCR 242 was passed as a basis for a "Just and Lasting Peace in the Middle East." Except for Iraq, which refused to accept the conditions but did not militarily continue to threaten Israel at the time, the war was essentially over.

The preemptive attack by Israel was launched while it was ostensibly at peace with the Arab nations. The opportunistic character of Nasser and the fact that large and modern Egyptian forces were deployed into the Sinai and West Bank, not to mention an offensive plan completed, though postponed, demonstrated the danger and imminence of the Egyptian attack. Israel's viable alternatives were one by one reduced due to Egyptian military action, arrangements completed for unified Arab command and control structure, and the failure of the United Nations to address any of the issues surrounding the build-

59

up of Egyptian forces in the Sinai. The legitimacy of their action was reflected in the relatively impartial resolutions passed in the United Nations Security Council and the support Israel received from the Western nations when attempts were made to affix the blame of aggression on them for the Six-Day War. The criterion established and met by Israel in the 1967 War is graphically depicted in table 3.

Table 3.   1967 Arab-Israeli War Analysis

| | | Self Defense – "Caroline Case" Webster | | | | |

Conflict	NSS Applicability	Imminence of Attack		No Viable Alternatives	Proportionality	Legitimacy
		Immediacy	Schmitt's "Last Window of Opportunity"			
1967 Arab-Israeli War	Conventional Warfare	☆		☆	☆	☆
Osirak Raid (Israel vs. Iraq)	WMD					
1982 Israeli invasion of Lebanon	Terrorism					

  Conditions for Criteria Met

  Conditions for Criteria Partially Met

The 1981 Israeli Raid on Osirak

Background

At 1600 local time, on 7 June 1981, eight newly purchased Israeli F-16s launched

from a base in the Sinai on a mission to destroy the al-Tuwaitha Nuclear reactor near

Baghdad, Iraq (see figure 2) (Grant 2002, 75). Reminiscent of the sale of M-48 tanks to

Jordan prior to the 1967 War, these F-16s had also been sold by the United States on the

condition that they would be used only for defense (Claire 2004, 118). The military

portion of the raid was highly successful, completely destroying the reactor core with no

losses in planes or pilots. The political impact was not as successful. See figure 5.

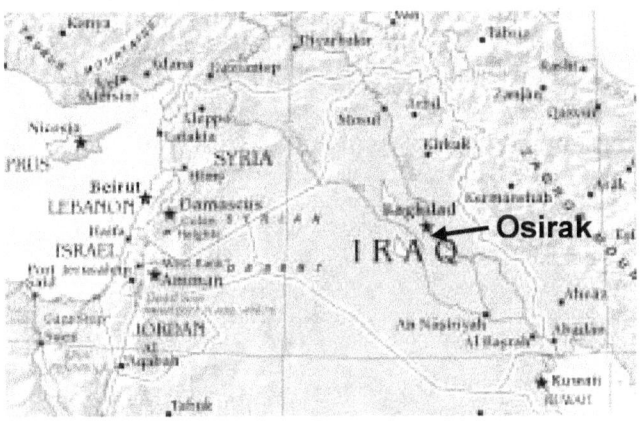

Figure 5.   Osirak

Source: CIA, *Fact Book*, 2005, available from http://www.cia.gov/cia/publications/
factbook/reference_maps/middle_east.html; Internet; accessed on 10 May 2005.

In 1974, shortly after the unsatisfactory end of the fourth Arab-Israeli War,

Saddam Hussein began negotiations for the purchase of a nuclear reactor during a state

visit to Iraq by the French Prime Minister, Jacques Chirac (Claire 2004, 38). Ostensibly

61

sold to the Iraqis for peaceful purposes, Israeli intelligence was convinced that Saddam Hussein had another idea in mind for the reactor; production of the "weapons grade plutonium" required building the first Arab nuclear weapon (Claire 2004, 95). To the Arabs it would be a counterweight to the nuclear weapons it was suspected that Israel already possessed in their arsenal (Claire 2004, 21). To the Israelis, juxtaposed on memories of the Holocaust and five Arab-Israeli wars, it once again invoked the specter of extermination. "Israel, whose population is largely concentrated in one or two urban areas, is particularly vulnerable to nuclear attack: one or two atomic warheads could deal the country a mortal blow" (Vandenbroucke 1984, 4).

This was seemingly confirmed after an Iranian air attack on Osirak in October 1980, when Hussein despite the ongoing war with Iran, reassured the Iranians that any weapons were "to be used against the Zionist enemies" (Grant 2002, 75). Significantly, a state of war was still ongoing since the Iraqis refused to sign the General Armistice Agreement with Israel in 1948.

Imminence

The timing of the attack on Osirak marked only the fuelling of the reactor, the actual production of enough plutonium to build two bombs would take another year (Claire 2004, 97). In purely military terms this meant that Iraq was not capable of conducting an imminent armed attack using nuclear weapons when the Israelis struck in June 1981 (McCoubrey and White 1992, 95). In retrospect the idea that Saddam Hussein would order the use of nuclear weapons if it were in his interests is indicated by his brutality toward his own people, even Ba'ath Party members (Claire 2004, 52), and the use of WMD against the Kurdish minority in Iraq. In the 1991 Gulf War, Iraq fired thirty-nine Scud missiles at Israel (Beres and Tsiddon-Chatto 1997, 1). The fact that he could order such an action, however, did not necessarily mean that he intended to launch a nuclear conflict (Crocket 2003, 17). However, the Israelis took a unique view of the imminence of the threat. It was not the actual creation of nuclear bombs that indicated an imminent threat; it was the activation of the reactor itself. Any attack on the facility after it was fueled could result in the deaths of hundred of thousands of Iraqis in the area (Claire 2004, 66). By slightly stretching Schmitt's concept, this allows the implication of the existence of a last window of opportunity, for the Israelis to strike prior to the fuelling of the facility in June 1981 (Claire 2004, 98). They had to destroy the facility, not only before it produced weapons to threaten Israel's major cities, but also before the mere act of destroying it could produce a nuclear catastrophe as well.

No Viable Alternatives

The Israelis had three alternatives; do nothing, use diplomatic efforts, or conduct a military strike. The first alternative would not be politically acceptable to the Israeli people or their Prime Minister, Menachem Begin. First, notwithstanding the existence of Israeli nuclear weapons, the fact of nuclear weapons in Iraq's hands upset the balance of power between the Arabs and Israelis. Second, Israeli elections were approaching and it was a possibility that Begin could be turned out of office.

> If Begin were to lose the prime ministry and a new government was formed, the opportunity to end Iraq's nuclear threat could be lost forever. The prime minister did not believe that Labor had the stomach to deal with the crisis. (Claire 2004, 99)

The Israelis actively approached other nations to delay or defeat the Iraqi nuclear efforts but were not satisfied with the answers they received. The United States

63

government, under both Presidents Carter and Ford, attempted to intervene with France to halt the nuclear exchange (Claire 2004, 40) and with Italy to prevent the sale of equipment that would assist the Iraqis in their nuclear projects (Claire 2004, 81). Both the French Premier and President were approached to reconsider the sale. Simon Peres personally appealed to Jacques Chirac and was put off (Claire 2004, 40). Begin wrote personally to Giscard d'Estaing asking that he halt further sales of uranium to Iraq and withdraw French technicians from the project but was also rebuffed (Claire 2004, 97). Finally, the Israelis achieved some success with the newly elected Francois Mitterrand, when he announced that France would no longer "engage in the sale of nuclear technology to Iraq" but "was bound to honor its present agreements" (Claire 2004, 147). Concurrent with the diplomatic offensive, the Israelis also allegedly engaged in sabotage (Claire 2004, 47) and assassination (Claire 2004, 65) attempts on Iraqi nuclear scientists working in France. As in 1967, the failure of the diplomatic alternative left in the Israeli estimation only the military one. "[W]e are faced with the greatest threat in the long history of Israel-annihilation and destruction of our country with atomic bomb by a madman terrorist who cares nothing for human life" (Claire 2004, 163).

Proportionality

The United States and the Soviet Union, large countries with diverse industrial centers, may have been able to survive a limited, if there is such a thing, nuclear exchange with a population and industrial base relatively intact. To Israel, however, even a limited nuclear exchange would be disastrous due to its small size and concentration of people. Offsetting the effect of a nuclear strike on Israel was the possible catastrophic effect of a strike on the reactor after it had been fuelled. A nuclear reaction, initiated by the bombing, would have killed "as many as one hundred thousand people" in close proximity to Baghdad (Claire 2004, 99). The loss of the reactor, prior to being fueled would render the entire complex harmless (Claire 2004, 101). That meant that the target was the reactor itself and stringent training was conducted to ensure that it was the only thing hit and bombs were not wasted on ancillary targets. The Israelis also attempted to limit casualties by attacking on a Sunday when they believed that the foreign technicians would not be at the site (Claire 2004, 99). As a result, only one French technician was killed in the raid (Claire 2004, 226).

Legitimacy

Despite diplomatic efforts prior to the attack, it cost them in the international arena, because the United States believed that Israel had deceived it, both in the purchase of the F-16s and in intelligence sharing agreements. However, the Israel leadership firmly believed it was acting in self-defense and that the use of the aircraft and intelligence was not a violation of their agreement with the United States. Despite the Israeli contention of an Iraqi nuclear threat, the United States immediately condemned "Israelis 'aggressive' and 'unprovoked' attack on Iraq" (Claire 2004, 220). The French too, outraged at the strike and the consequent death of a French Citizen, called the attack "unacceptable, dangerous and a serious violation of international law" (Claire 2004, 227). In fact, the attack resulted in the passage of United Nations Resolution 487, supported by the United States, condemning Israel for "violation of the United Nations Charter and the norms of international law" (Claire 2004, 229). The Reagan administration was deeply concerned about the violation of the sales restriction and the message it sent the Arabs about the conditions in their weapons sales agreements with the United States (Claire 2004, 219).

65

Clearly, in the absence of an imminent threat of attack and based on the supposition that Iraq might be building a nuclear weapon that they might someday use against Israel, the attack on Osirak was a preventive and not a preemptive attack. Finally, in the eyes of the world as demonstrated by the passage of Resolution 487, the attack was not a legitimate act. Unlike the aftermath of the 1967 War, the United States did not support Israel's attack on Osirak. By not even discussing the possibility of an attack with the United States and then failing to notify their "closest ally" (Claire 2004, 102), the Israelis failed partially to shape American reaction in a favorable manner. Instead, the United States was blindsided by the attack on Iraq, who the United States was supporting in their war with Iran, forced to choose between allies, and essentially were left with no choice but to condemn Israel. The criteria met by Israel in the attack on Osirak are graphically depicted in table 4.

Table 4.   1981 Raid on Osirak Analysis

Conflict	NSS Applicability	Imminence of Attack		No Viable Alternatives	Proportionality	Legitimacy
		Immediacy	Schmitt's "Last Window of Opportunity"			
1967 Arab-Israeli War	Conventional Warfare	✸		✸	✸	✸
Osirak Raid (Israel vs. Iraq)	WMD		✸	✸	✸	
1982 Israeli invasion of Lebanon	Terrorism					

Self Defense – "Caroline Case" Webster

  Conditions for Criteria Met

  Conditions for Criteria Partially Met

The 1982 Israeli Invasion of Lebanon

Background

By 1982, Lebanon was a sovereign state in name only. The Syrians controlled most of Northern and Western Lebanon down to the Bekaa Valley. The PLO, "substituting its own administrative authority for the Lebanese political, economic, and administrative systems," controlled a large portion from Beirut to the Litani River (Dupuy and Martell 1986, 47). The United Nations Interim Force in Lebanon (UNIFIL) had established a protected zone between the PLO occupied areas and a buffer zone known as Free Lebanon, run by an allegedly renegade Lebanese Major Haddad. Except for some areas of Beirut and the Christian Maronite areas just to the north, the Lebanese Government could not exercise control within its legally recognized borders. In 1968, despite being a signatory of the 1949 armistice with Israel and under pressure from fellow Arab nations, Lebanon had allowed the PLO to establish bases in southern Lebanon (Laffin 1985, 9). These bases expanded significantly when King Hussein expelled the PLO from Jordan in 1970. Disillusioned by the failure of the Arab states to defeat Israel, or even to maintain unity in support of the Palestinian cause, the PLO began to build a more conventional force to fight the Israelis (Davis 1987, 43). From the time of their movement into Lebanon, cross border operations and artillery duels began taking place, resulting in the deaths of civilians, both in Lebanon and Galilee (see figure 6), the most northern province of Israel. In response to these incidents, the Israelis conducted multiple attacks into Lebanon to remove the PLO threat, most notably in the 1978 Operation Litani, that resulted in the passage of UNSCR 425 and the introduction of UNIFIL as a buffer. Accepted by Israel, the resolution was rejected by Yasir Arafat because "there is no cease-fire in the vocabulary of the Palestinian revolution" (Dupuy and Martell 1986, 50). Despite the introduction of UNIFIL, the attacks did not cease. "Between June and December 1980 alone there were 69 successful infiltrations by terrorists through the UNIFIL zone" (Laffin 1985, 18). In May 1981, the PLO fired 1230 artillery salvoes killing 26 people and wounding 59 (Laffin 1985, 18). The Israelis again retaliated, initiating an offensive against the PLO in Lebanon that only ended with a cease-fire negotiated by Philip Habib, a United States Ambassador of Lebanese extraction. Both sides interpreted this cease-fire differently; the Israelis believed that all hostilities would be halted, while the Palestinians insisted that it only applied along the Israeli-Lebanese

68

border, a crucial and ominous difference of opinion (Dupuy and Martell 1986, 83). Not trusting the PLO and "shortly after the July 1981 cease-fire in Lebanon, the Israeli government began planning to invade Lebanon" (Davis 1987, 66). The PLO did maintain the ceasefire along the border, but continued its operations elsewhere. From 24 July 1981, the date of the cease-fire mediated by Ambassador Habib, there were over 209 "separate attacks on Israel, Israelis abroad, the West Bank, and Maj. Haddad's enclaves" resulting in 29 deaths (Laffin 1985, 24). On 4 August 1981, shortly after the cease-fire agreement was signed, Ariel Sharon was appointed Minister of Defense (Davis 1987, 65). A successful General in the 1973 War against Egypt, he was convinced that "sooner or later Israel would have no choice but to 'take decisive military action' against the PLO in Lebanon" (Laffin 1985, 20). Sharon also believed that to destroy the PLO, the Israelis would have to cut Beirut off from Syrian support. He either never informed the Israeli Prime Minister, Menachem Begin, of this or Begin withheld it because Israel's "announced aim was to clear a zone extending 40 kilometers north of its border" (Davis 1987, 11).

Between 9 May and 3 June 1982, the PLO had conducted twenty-eight attacks in Israel and on Israelis abroad, culminating in the final spark that set off the Israeli invasion, the attack on the Israeli Ambassador to the United Kingdom on 3 June (Dupuy and Martell 1986, 94). In retaliation on 4 June, Israel launched a major air attack against PLO positions in Lebanon and Beirut. The PLO responded with an artillery barrage, followed immediately by further Israeli attacks (Davis 1987, 75). On 5 June, as heavy artillery shelling of Galilee continued, the Israeli cabinet gave the defense minister permission to cross the border (Davis 1987, 77). At 11:00 AM, 6 June, three columns totaling nine divisional equivalents crossed the border into Lebanon and the war was hot

again (Davis 1987, 77). See figure6.

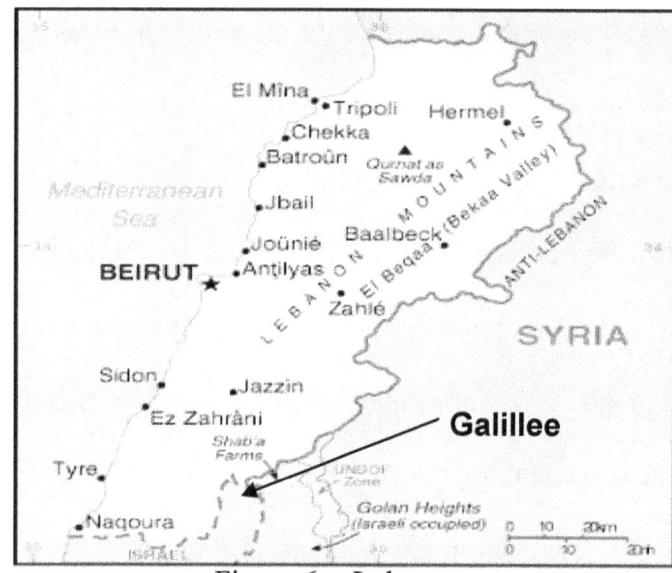

Figure 6.   Lebanon

Source: CIA, *Fact Book*, 2005, available from http://www.cia.gov/cia/publications/
factbook/reference_maps/middle_east.html; Internet; accessed on 10 May 2005.

Imminence

The question of imminence in the 1982 Invasion of Lebanon is rendered moot by

the ongoing nature of the conflict despite the cease-fire negotiated previously by

Ambassador Habib. The PLO was not going to attack Israel; they were already attacking

Israel at home and abroad. The PLO's interpretation was that the agreement only

pertained to the Israeli-Lebanese border and that they could conduct operations elsewhere

ensured that the hostilities would continue. The PLO was strengthening its hold on

southern Lebanon, building a conventional force to defend its holdings and to participate

in the next Arab-Israeli War. By 1982, this force was to have approximately eighty tanks,

70

mainly obsolete T-34/55 Soviet tanks, and a substantial amount of more modern artillery including ninety 133-millimeter and 155-millimeter guns, eighty BM-21 122-millimeter launchers and 200 heavy mortars (Laffin 1985, 30). To operate these and provide infantry support were "about 15,000 regular fighters organized into battalions" and "18,000 militiamen recruited from among Palestinian refugees" (Laffin 1985, 30). The "PLO was building in southern Lebanon, a large conventional army and was preparing to make the switch from guerilla to conventional arms in its confrontation with Israel" (Davis 1987, 111). The PLO's actual conventional combat capability was no match to the Israelis at that point but they were building a state that could exercise all of the elements of state power.

No Viable Alternatives

In accordance with UNSCR 425, Israel had turned over to UNIFIL most of the territory occupied in the 1978 invasion under the assumption that the United Nations would then prevent PLO infiltration of the northern border. It was a bad assumption; instead the area controlled by the United Nations became a haven for the PLO (Laffin 1985, 20). The United Nations Security Council had passed resolutions calling for the end of the cross-border firing by both sides, and the UNIFIL Commander arrived at the Northern Headquarters to discuss the resolutions minutes before the attack was launched (Laffin 1985, 20). The Soviet Union and Syria were providing arms, intelligence, and military advice to the PLO. The PLO refused to amend their establishing covenant that rejected the existence of Israel and any solution that didn't include the "total liberation of Palestine" (Bavly and Salpeter 1984, 18). The total liberation of Palestine correspondingly meant the total elimination of the state of Israel. The 3 June attack on

Ambassador Argov was made by followers of Abu Nidal whose organization was only loosely under the command of Yasir Arafat and the PLO (Davis 1987, 44). The assassination attempt however, provided the necessary pretext to launch the invasion. The resulting alternatives were to do nothing and continue the low-level warfare with the PLO; invade and push the PLO back into Lebanon far enough to ensure that their weapons could not range Israeli settlements; or the third option was to attempt to destroy the PLO's military infrastructure in Lebanon. In the preceding year, the Israelis had actually mobilized on the northern border four times but had not invaded Lebanon (Dupuy and Martell 1986, 81). This time Ariel Sharon meant to remove the problem completely.

Proportionality

The Israelis invaded initially to establish a 40-kilometer barrier between the PLO and their artillery and rocket positions and the settlements in northern Israel. It was supposed to be a war focused on the PLO and assurances were given "that a clash with the Syrians would be avoided at all costs" (Davis 1987, 116). Both of these factors indicated proportionality in planning the invasion, limited in scope with limited objectives. The actual invasion was not, however, proportional to the artillery and rocket attacks. Instead, it was an attempt to destroy the Palestinian organization in Lebanon, an impossible task to assign to the IDF, even by Israeli standards. "The former Chief of Military Intelligence, Major General Shlomo Gazit, had stated earlier that as a terrorist and organization and political phenomenon the PLO could be controlled, but not destroyed: It could only be dealt with effectively through a political solution" (Davis 1987, 113).

72

The nine division sized force was too big to clear the 40-kilometer buffer zone and too small to accomplish everything Sharon expected of it (Davis 1987, 113). Despite the assurances that Syria was not to be attacked, the destruction of their allies, and sometimes proxies, the PLO in the internecine fighting amongst Lebanese factions made war with them a distinct probability (Dupuy and Martell 1986, 81). This is not what was sold to President Reagan, the world, or even the Israeli people.

Legitimacy

That Israel had a right to act in self-defense against the PLO artillery attacks is established by the Corfu Case in that the Government of Lebanon could not prevent the PLO from launching attacks on Israel from Lebanese territory (Dinstein 2001, 214). Where the Begin Government failed was in not shaping the political conditions prior to the invasion and in the proportionality of the invasion itself. Relations with the United States were still strained from the 1981 attack on the Osirak Nuclear Plant in Iraq, for which the Israelis were condemned in the United Nations Security Council (Davis 1987, 64). These relations were to remain under duress until Begin resigned from office in 1983 (Davis 1987, 117). Begin had destroyed budding relations with France in the aftermath of Osirak, by publicly rejecting Prime Minister Mitterrand's call for a Palestinian state (Davis 1987, 69). The PLO believed that an attack by Israel would be an international political success for the Palestinian cause, demonstrating that the Israelis were the aggressors and that the PLO were the protectors of the downtrodden, completely reversing the roles played by the Arabs and Israel in the previous four wars (Dupuy and Martell 1986, 81). Israeli public opinion, initially supported the war, but gradually turned against the war and the government as the IDF passed the 40-kilometer mark and conflict commenced with the Syrians in western Lebanon. The Israelis lost further American support when it was reported that they were using cluster bombs "in violation of sales agreements" (Davis 1987, 84). For a small state, surrounded by enemies and under the constant threat of terror attacks, it was imperative to avoid isolation by the international community (Davis 1987, 44). Israel failed in this when, on 6 June, the United Nations Security Council passed a resolution calling for the immediate withdrawal of Israel from Lebanon and two days later the United States vetoed a resolution that would have placed sanctions on Israel (Davis 1987, 90). If the Israelis had stayed with their announced intention of clearing up to the 40-kilometer mark, the first resolution might have also been vetoed by the United States. In fact, the Israelis timed the attack to prevent the United States from intervening and pressuring the Begin Government not to attack (Davis 1987, 78). The Security Council was taking action, a resolution to stop the shelling had been passed and the UNIFIL Commander was attempting to coordinate efforts to execute those resolutions and stop the cross-border attacks. The Israeli leadership was not listening. The legitimacy of the invasion of Lebanon is reflected on the table 5.

Table 5.   1982 Invasion of Lebanon Analysis

Conflict	NSS Applicability	Imminence of Attack		No Viable Alternatives	Proportionality	Legitimacy
		Immediacy	Schmitt's "Last Window of Opportunity"			
1967 Arab-Israeli War	Conventional Warfare	✳		✳	✳	✳
Osirak Raid (Israel vs. Iraq)	WMD		✳	✳	✳	
1982 Israeli invasion of Lebanon	Terrorism	✳				

Self Defense – "Caroline Case" Webster

 Conditions for Criteria Met

 Conditions for Criteria Partially Met

Conclusion

Each of the above case studies evaluates the strategy of preemption as practiced

by the State of Israel against different types of threats determined by their government to

threaten the continued existence of the state. Each of these types of threat is now believed

to be aimed at the United States as indicated by their inclusion in the Bush

administration's *NSS* of 2002. Each case study examines the sufficient and necessary

conditions that the Israeli Government believed to exist prior to their taking military

action to defeat the threat and whether the international community, as indicated by the

resolutions of the United Nations Security Council, considered it legitimate. The 1967

75

War case study evaluates a preemptive strike against a conventional threat. Because the Israelis successfully shaped the political environment prior to taking action, it was a legitimate act of preemption. Despite efforts by the United States to restrain Israel prior to the action, it prevented the passage of resolutions in the Security Council condemning Israel after the fact. In the second case study, the Israeli Government failed to shape the political environment prior to the raid on the Iraqi nuclear facility at Osirak. In the aftermath of the attack, the United States, the primary military and political ally of Israel, joined the international community in condemning the action. The third case study was the 1982 Israeli invasion of Lebanon, which once again demonstrated the importance of shaping the international environment even in a preemptive act against terrorists. In this case, the actions of the Begin Government resulted in the international isolation of Israel and the passage of resolutions demanding their immediate withdrawal from Lebanon. Significantly, although the United States agreed to the resolutions on withdrawal, it blocked any attempts by the Security Council to place sanctions on Israel. Each case study dealt with a threat that the United States faces today and is addressed by the *NSS* of 2002, emergence of a peer threat, WMD, and terrorism. The significant difference is that the United States, for the most part, was able to minimize the international effects of Israel's actions by vetoing, or threatening to veto, Security Council Resolutions that would have significantly impacted the Israeli economy and the readiness of its military forces. The United States, in its turn, may veto, or threaten to veto, resolutions directed at its actions but the resulting failure of legitimacy also influences the necessary political and material support provided by other nations in the aftermath of those actions. By studying the international political reaction generated by Israel's preemptive acts, the

United States may be able to better shape the political environment and avoid those same

pitfalls, resulting in acceptance and legitimacy by the international community.

CHAPTER 5

CONCLUSION

It is very dangerous to precipitate an action when a little patience
would create a reasonable hope of changing the form of war to
advantage.

Jay Luvass, *Frederick the Great*

A war of invasion without good reason-like that of Genghis Khan-
is a crime against humanity; but it may be excused, if not
approved, when induced by great interests or when conducted with
good motives.

Antoine Jomini, *Roots of Strategy, Book 2*

Introduction

The Israeli experience with preemptive attacks was a mixed bag of results in

terms of both tactical and strategic effects and, as a result, is instructive for the adoption

of a preemptive strategy as a cornerstone of United States Foreign policy. The 1981

attack on the Iraqi Osirak nuclear facility at al-Tuwaitha cost the Israeli Government

international legitimacy and resulted in condemnation by the United Nations Security

Council and Israel's chief sponsor, the United States. The 1982 invasion of Lebanon,

while succeeding in preempting attacks from southern Lebanon, drew them into a twenty-

year occupation mission that not only cost them international legitimacy but also

domestically resulted in the fall of Menachem Begin's Government. The case studies

below, involving the interests of the United States directly, will use the same framework

for discussion as in the Israeli case studies; imminence of attack, no viable alternatives,

and proportionality. Included under imminence of attack will be Schmitt's concept of last

window of opportunity. Finally, the legitimacy of an attack will be evaluated by the public policies adopted by the five permanent members of the United Nations Security Council. In the first case study, the 2003 United States invasion of Iraq, the public statements leading up to the war and their participation in it will serve to confirm, or not, the legitimacy of the action. In the following two case studies involving potential future conflicts against North Korea and Iran, the public policies will also be used but included will be an evaluation of how the United States is shaping, or needs to shape, the international environment in pursuing a preemptive strategy against those nations.

2003 United States Invasion of Iraq

Background

On 2 August 1990, Saddam Hussein invaded the small but oil-rich nation of Kuwait. Located strategically in the Persian Gulf, the territory now called Kuwait had once been part of Iraq. They had been separated by the decision of the British colonial power; however, Iraq continued to refer to Kuwait as an Iraqi Province. The casus belli for the invasion was the alleged illegal drilling by Kuwait into underground oil fields that extended into Iraqi territory, but the real reason for the invasion was the wealth of Kuwait (Keegan 2004, 7). Saddam had bankrupted his country in a disastrous eight-year war with Iran in the 1980's. In less than six months, the United Nations had passed twelve resolutions increasingly insistent that Iraq withdraw from Kuwait, culminating in Resolution 687 on 29 November 1990 that authorized the application of all necessary means to remove Iraqi Forces from Kuwait if they had not withdrawn by 15 January 1991 (Keegan 2004, 76). On 17 January 1991, the American-led coalition began a month-long air war that culminated in a four-day ground war that drove Hussein's forces ignominiously out of Kuwait. Hussein's defeat precipitated the revolt of the Shia population of southern Iraq. As the world watched, Saddam Hussein brutally crushed this revolt, with the full horror only revealed in 2003 when coalition forces discovered the multiplicity of mass graves dating from this period (Keegan 2004, 83). The Gulf War, however, was far from over. See figure 7.

Figure 7.   Iraq

Source: CIA, *Fact Book*, 2005, available from http://www.cia.gov/cia/publications/ factbook/reference_maps/middle_east.html; Internet; accessed on 10 May 2005.

In the aftermath of the war, an inspections regime was established by United Nations Security Resolution 687 to ensure the dismantling of Iraq's WMD program which had caused so much concern prior to the coalition's attack into Kuwait (Blix 2003). To keep the pressure on Hussein to cooperate with the inspections, the United

Nations put economic sanctions in place and the coalition established no-fly zones, first in southern Iraq and later in the north. As a result, for the next twelve years, American and British pilots patrolled the skies over Iraq, and in "nearly every mission they had been fired on or threatened by the Iraqi air defense system" (Woodward 2004, 10). On at least two occasions, all-out air offensives were launched to punish the Hussein for his repeated intransigence in complying with United Nations resolutions and the attempted assassination of former President George H. W. Bush in 1993. Hussein's failure to comply with United Nations Security Council Resolutions was the casus belli for the United States invasion in 2003. Since 1991, "Iraq had been found guilty of material breach of its obligations stretching back over 16 previous resolutions" (Powell 2003). United Nations inspections had been taking place for eight years after the cease-fire but Iraq's cooperation throughout was characterized as "often withheld or given grudgingly" (Blix 2003). In 1998 even Hussein's grudging cooperation ended when, upon Iraqi insistence, the inspectors were withdrawn, precipitating United States and United Kingdom air strikes in December 1998, known as Operation Desert Fox. After seven years of air strikes, United States policy towards Iraq began to change from the long-term strategy of containment in favor of a policy of regime change. In 1998 Congress passed, and President Clinton signed into law a bill that "authorized up to $97 million in military assistance to Iraqi opposition forces to remove the regime headed by Saddam Hussein' and ' promote the emergence of a democratic government'" (Woodward 2004, 10). It was also in 1998 when a letter to President Clinton was published, concluding that the strategy of containment pursued against Iraq was eroding and warned of the danger posed by Saddam Hussein developing WMD. The signers, including Richard Armitage, Donald

81

Rumsfeld, and Paul Wolfowitz, believed that the United States had the "authority under existing UN resolutions to take the necessary steps, including military steps, to protect our vital interests in the Gulf. In any case, American policy cannot continue to be crippled by a misguided insistence on unanimity in the UN Security Council" (Abrams et al. 1998, 2).

Between 1998 and 2003, two events in the United States set the stage for the invasion of Iraq, first was the election of George W. Bush, son of the former United States President that Saddam Hussein had allegedly tried to assassinate, and second, the terrorist attack on 11 September 2001. The second President Bush's administration included many who had worked for his father during the 1991 Gulf War, including Dick Cheney, now Vice President and then Secretary of Defense, Colin Powell now Secretary of State and then CJCS, and Paul Wolfowitz, then Undersecretary of Defense for Policy and now Deputy Secretary of Defense. After the terrorist attacks on 11 September, Wolfowitz was already thinking about Iraq and for Cheney at least, the removal of Saddam Hussein became almost an obsession (Woodward 2004, 4). The President himself was already thinking in terms of war with Iraq barely two months after the terrorist attack and while still in the throes of the war in Afghanistan (Woodward 2004, 1). President Bush articulates the "why" for this in the *NSS* of 2002, "We must be prepared to stop rogue states *and their terrorist clients* [Emphasis mine] before they are able to threaten or use weapons of mass destruction against the United States and our allies and friends" (U.S. President 2002, 14). In the President's mind, the possibility of a link between required the United States to take action to prevent a nuclear, biological, or chemical 11 September.

Imminence

The case made before the United Nations by the United States Secretary of State, Colin L. Powell, was principally a legal one in that Iraq had ignored United Nations Security Council resolutions for twelve years and had been "repeatedly convicted over the years" by the Security Council with numerous resolutions. In fact, the case was an attempt by the United States to force the United Nations to come to grips with the Iraq issue, if it refused to "It will be impotent and have to do it on our own" (Woodward 2004, 308). In October of 2002, the Director for Central Intelligence published a report that Iraq already had biological warfare agents and was "capable of quickly producing and weaponizing a variety of agents, including anthrax, for delivery by bombs, missiles, aerial sprayers, and covert operatives, including potentially against the US Homeland" (Director of Central Intelligence 2002, 2). The same report also stated that:

> If Baghdad acquires sufficient weapons-grade fissile material from abroad, it could make a nuclear weapon within a year. Without such material from abroad, Iraq probably would not be able to make a weapon until the last half of the decade. (Director of Central Intelligence 2002, 1)

It would take at least a year for Iraq to build a nuclear weapon, if they could acquire enough fissile material (in other words uranium 235) to make such a weapon feasible. However, the crux of the matter for the Bush administration was the potential threat to the homeland of the United States as Doctor Rice stated to CNN, "We don't want the smoking gun to be a mushroom cloud" (Woodward 2004, 179). It was then with this picture in mind that the Secretary of State drew the connection between Iraq and terror for the Security Council and underlined the American necessity for attacking Iraq. "Terrorism has been a tool used by Saddam for decades. Saddam was a supporter of terrorism long before these new terrorist networks had a name, and this support continues. The nexus of poisons and terror is new. The nexus of terror and Iraq is old. The combination is lethal" (Powell 2003). Despite Powell's brilliant presentation of the threat to the Security Council regarding the connection between Iraq and terror and Powell's was not a case describing an imminent attack on the United States by Iraq, but a case for maintaining the relevancy of the United Nations by enforcing its resolutions on a malevolent and incompliant rogue state.

What undercuts the imminence of the threat, however, is that members of the Bush administration were clearly thinking in terms of military action to remove the threat of WMD, Saddam Hussein or both as early as 1998 (Abrams et.al. 1998, 2).

No Viable Alternatives

The United States had two viable alternatives. First, continue with diplomacy and the containment of Iraq, and second invade to effect regime change. President Clinton's administration established regime change as United States policy. Since 1991, there had been ten UNSCR regarding Iraq and Hussein's failure to adhere to the original requirements of the ceasefire with the coalition. The eleventh, and final, Security Council Resolution 1441 passed in November of 2002. This resolution, in the words of Secretary Powell, gave the Iraqis one last chance to "come into compliance or face serious consequences" (2003). Significantly, this was not the same wording found in the UNSCR in 1991, which authorized the United States-led coalition to use all necessary means to evict Saddam Hussein from Kuwait. However, it did succeed in getting the inspection program reinstated and United Nations weapons inspectors back into Iraq. Concurrent with the diplomatic efforts was the military containment of Iraq by coalition forces. According to a previous Commander of United States Central Command, the policy of containment was working. The Iraqi military was half the size it had been during the 1991 Gulf War and what was left consisted of "obsolete equipment, ill-trained troops, dissatisfaction in the ranks, a lot of absenteeism" and his remaining WMD were aging artillery shells and rocket rounds (Zinni 2004). However, the report from the Executive Chairman of the United Nations Monitoring, Verification and Inspection Commission (UNMOVIC), while going to great lengths not to confirm the existence of WMD in Iraq, went to just as great lengths not to confirm its absence. In fact, Doctor Blix reports the renovation and repair of facilities destroyed by UNMOVIC's predecessor, the United Nations Special Committee (UNSCOM) that was expelled by Iraq in 1998. UNSCOM's Director, Richard Butler, believed that "Iraq's behavior in respect of its obligations, principally under Security Council resolution 687, has also raised very grave challenges to both the authority of the Security Council and to the credibility of efforts to verify compliance with the non-proliferation regimes." In determining whether there were other viable options available, one must remember Dinstein's caution that the facts must be judged as known at the time of decision and not by subsequently revealed knowledge or hindsight.

Proportionality

By all accounts, the Iraqi Army as an effective fighting force was significantly diminished from the forty divisions that the coalition faced in 1991. In 2003, it consisted of only 17 badly equipped and administered divisions with only 2,000 aging tanks, little more than 2,000 artillery pieces of all types, less than 2,000 armored personnel carriers, and at best estimates only 200,000 men (Keegan 2004, 129). It was a mere shadow of the army of 1991 and "less than half its size from the beginning of the Gulf War" (Zinni

2004). To face this army, the coalition fielded four reinforced divisions, including one Marine and one British, which were qualitatively superior to the Iraqi formations, including M1A2 Abrams tanks and Bradley fighting vehicles (Keegan 2004, 129). Significantly, the Coalition had air supremacy over Iraq even before the beginning of the war. In 1991, the Iraqi Air Force ignominiously and sensibly "decamped en masse to Iran, where it was given refuge until the war was over" (Keegan 2004, 129). Since then the Iraqi Air Force was of little to no note in preventing the coalition aircraft from entering its air space at will.

What did concern the leaders of the coalition were the stocks of unaccounted WMD. The Executive Chairman of UNMOVIC, Doctor Hans Blix, assumed there were unaccounted for weapons in his report to the Security Council on 27 January 2003. In his mind, there were discrepancies of 6,500 chemical bombs containing 1,000 tons of chemical agent, several thousand chemical rockets, and higher than reported stocks of weaponized VX nerve agent and the biological warfare agent anthrax (Powell 2003). In addition to the discrepancy in chemical agents that might be available, Iraq was also working on rockets, the Al Samoud 2 and the Al Fatah, which had ranges in excess of the 150-kilometers allowed under UNSCR 687 (Powell 2003). The existence of these chemicals was determined by reviewing Iraq's own records on development and, in some cases, destruction. In President Bush's mind, the proportionality of the threat was underlined in his speech to the American people on the reasons for going to war. "We meet this threat now, with our Army, Air Force, Navy, Coast Guard and Marines, so that we do not have to meet them later with armies of firefighters and police and doctors in the streets of our cities" (Woodward 2004, 179). Finally, Iraq failed to comply with twelve previous United Nations Security Council Resolutions that required it to divest itself of WMD and their failure to cooperate fully with resolution 1441 indicated that Saddam Hussein would continue to do so in the future. In the end, the Bush Administration came to the same conclusion that the Clinton Administration reached, that regime change was the only way to ensure that Iraq was WMD free.

Legitimacy

The discussion of legitimacy in the 2003 Iraq invasion is complicated by the lack of an actual vote in the Security Council to quantitatively demonstrate the positions of the five permanent members; however, their public statements can infer their positions if a vote had been brought before the Security Council. The United States clearly believed that the passage of UNSCR 1441 on 8 November 2002, found Iraq "guilty of a material breach of its obligations" to destroy not only its stocks WMD but also the program that produced them (Powell 2003). The resolution had been adopted unanimously, including the surprising vote of Syria, but there was a serious difference in terminology between 1441 and the resolution passed to authorize the 1991 Gulf War (Woodward 2004, 226). 1441 stated, "if Saddam Hussein continued to violate his disarmament obligations, he would face 'serious consequences'" (Woodward 2004, 226). The 1991 Security Council Resolution used the phrase "all necessary means" to authorize military action (Woodward 2004, 226). Colin Powell introduced this slight, but significant, difference to get the support of the other five permanent members. In effect, it meant that the United States would have to get a second Security Council resolution specifically authorizing the use of force. Resolution 1441 required Iraq to accept the resolution within seven days, report the status of their WMD programs to the Security Council within thirty days, and allow

United Nations weapons inspectors back into the country. Iraq partially, but not completely, complied with all of the requirements (Keegan 2004, 110). It accepted the resolution and allowed the weapons inspectors back in. However, their reception and lack of complete cooperation reflected the delaying tactics used against UNSCOM. In addition, the report on the progress of disarmament was not accepted by the United States, "Iraq's non-compliance and defiance of the international community has brought it closer to the day when he [Saddam Hussein] has to face the consequences. This declaration fails totally to move us in the direction of a peaceful solution" (Keegan 2004, 110). While the United States declared it a "material breach," Prime Minister Blair of the United Kingdom was faced with anti-war demonstrations and a reluctance of his government to go to war without a second resolution (Keegan 2004, 115). It was with this in mind that Secretary of State Colin Powell went back to the Security Council to present the case against Iraq and get the authorization. Despite some initial optimism that the case was made to the international community, the leaders of France, Russia, and Germany "issued a strong joint statement the same day calling for extended weapons inspections. 'Nothing today justifies war,' Chirac said. Russia, Germany and France are determined to ensure that everything possible is done to disarm Iraq peacefully" (Woodward 2004, 315). Three of the five permanent members had now made their positions plain on taking action against Iraq; the United States in favor while Russia and France stood against. China, like Russia and France, having "close commercial ties to Iraq," had also spoken out against unilateral American action (Woodward 2004, 222). However, they had abstained on the resolution in 1991, and in view of developing relations with the West might abstain again or even vote in favor of a resolution to take

88

more direct measures against Iraq (Keegan 2004, 115). In the United Kingdom, the Attorney General ruled that a material breach of Resolution 687, requiring the destruction of all WMD and means of delivery, such as missiles, revived authority to use force under 687. In Resolution 1441, "the UN determined that Iraq has been and remains in material breach of Resolution 687" (Keegan 2004, 123-4). Despite some resignations from his government, this ruling gave Blair the moral authority to support a second resolution in the Security Council, should one be put for a vote. Support for a second resolution now stood at two in favor, two against, and one abstention. Despite these numbers, diplomacy continued until on 10 March Jacques Chirac "announced that France would vote against, whatever the circumstances" (Keegan 2004, 122). Clearly, no resolution authorizing an attack on Iraq was going to be passed by the Security Council. More problematic for the United States and the United Kingdom, however, were the old allies who voted with their feet by not providing troops for the invasion or security operations afterwards. The criteria established and met by the United States for the 2003 invasion of Iraq is graphically depicted in table 6.

Table 6.   The 2003 Invasion of Iraq Analysis

Conflict	NSS Applicability	Imminence of Attack		No Viable Alternatives	Proportionality	Legitimacy
		Immediacy	Schmitt's "Last Window of Opportunity"			
2003 US invasion of Iraq	Conventional Warfare					
North Korea	Nexus of WMD and Terrorism					
Iran	Terrorism					

Self Defense – "Caroline Case" Webster

  Conditions for Criteria Met

  Conditions for Criteria Partially Met

North Korea

Background

On 25 June 1950, North Korean troops crossed the 38th Parallel inaugurating an indecisive war that caused the combatants almost three million casualties (Stoessinger 2001, 75). Taking advantage of a Soviet boycott of the United Nations, the United States put together a Security Council authorized coalition to "push the communists back above the 38th parallel" (Nye 2003, 123). In 1953, after three years of bitter fighting, an armistice was finally concluded at Panmunjom (Dinstein 2001, 138). The war did not end; however, and in the absence of a formal peace treaty, the armies remain facing each

90

other across a demilitarized zone (Stoessinger 2001, 76). Instead, the adversaries on the Korean Peninsula remained in a stalemate, conducting perpetual armistice talks framed by the wider conflict of the Cold War between the United States and the Soviet Union. Despite numerous small and deadly infiltration operations conducted by the North into the South, the situation remained tense but stable until 1989 when North Korea's chief sponsor, the Soviet Union dissolved. Caught up in its own domestic turmoil, now, Russia no longer could afford to subsidize the North Korean government and the North Korean economy made a drastic turn for the worse (*Chronology* 2005). The worsening economy is a critical factor in North Korea's foreign policy; they desperately needed hard currency to keep their country afloat. One of the ways to keep their economy afloat was the sale of missile technology, which became "a substantial source of hard currency earnings to them" (Carter 2002, 9). The North Koreans sold missiles to anyone who would buy them, including Pakistan, Syria, Egypt, and Iran (Carter 2002, 8).

In 1985, North Korea signed the Nuclear Non-Proliferation Treaty (NPT) but did not allow IAEA inspectors in until seven years later. In a scene to be repeated eight years later in Iraq, when the team, also led by Hans Blix, finally did get in they found evidence that the North Koreans were "not revealing the full extent of its plutonium production" (*Chronology* 2005). Less than a year later in 1993, Hans Blix states that he can no longer "provide 'any meaningful assurances' that North Korea is not producing nuclear weapons" (*Chronology* 2005). It is clear that, WMD has become a bargaining tool for the North Korean Regime. The United States makes offers to provide equipment, food, and fuel in exchange for the halting and eventual dismantling of the weapons program. The North Koreans would initially agree only to later make stipulations that would require further inducements, both political and economic, before they would adhere to their non-proliferation commitments under the NPT. In the two-party negotiations, Pyongyang held all of the cards. International pressure and inducements did not seem to be effective. Nor were threats by the United States to attack because of North Korea's threats to turn Seoul into a "sea of flames" (*Chronology* 2005, 2). In 1994, North Korea and the United States created the "Agreed Framework" in which the United States, Japan, and South Korea would provide heavy fuel oil and, eventually, light water reactors. In return, North Korea would cease plutonium processing and close their nuclear research facilities (Frontline: Kim's Nuclear Gamble 2005b, 3). Despite intense criticism in the United States that the Clinton Administration was the victim of nuclear blackmail, both sides adhered essentially to the letter of the agreement. The letter was important because it only specified plutonium processing. "They didn't say anything about uranium" (Frontline: Kim's Nuclear Gamble 2005b, 3, 9). The North Koreans did not address missile development either and caught the world by surprise in 1998 when it fired a Taepodong missile over the Sea of Japan. The development of delivery means raised the stakes considerably and proved that North Korea had the capability to hit Japan (*Chronology* 2005, 4). In 2002, the CIA reported that North Korea was pursuing a program to enrich uranium, technically not in violation of the Agreed Framework because it was not plutonium (*Chronology* 2005, 8). In 2005, North Korea achieved the ability to "arm a missile with a nuclear device" (Graham and Kessler 2005, 1). Realizing that without North Korea's major sponsors involved in any negotiations, the Bush Administration proposes a framework of multilateral talks, involving North Korea's major trading partners China and Russia to increase the likelihood that North Korea will abide by its

agreements (*Chronology* 2005, 8).

In the background of the political process, there was a huge humanitarian disaster

unfolding in North Korea,

> A combination of long term economic decline and devastating weather conditions
> lead to a famine during the mid-1990s, during which foreign aid workers estimate
> as many as 2 million people die[d] of starvation. In 1995-6 floods destroy 16-
> percent of the country's arable land. In 1997 and again in 2000, North Korea
> suffers a devastating drought along its fertile West Coast. According to the World
> Food Programme, the food deficit in North Korea has been in excess of 1 million
> tons per year since 1995. (*Chronology* 2005, 8)

This contributes to regime instability that threatens neighboring countries. If the regime

fell, China and South Korea would potentially have to deal with "thousands of refugees

over the border into China" in addition to the already "tens of thousands of North

Koreans who are believed to be living in and traveling to and from China" (Manyin, et al.

2005, CRS-3). Of additional concern to all, and specifically the United States, would be

the status of any nuclear weapons or fissile material and their disposition in order to keep

them out of the wrong hands. With the back ground established, what would the

conditions need to look like for the United States to conduct a preemptive strike either

against an imminent attack by North Korea, or, in terms of a last window of opportunity,

the imminent transfer of WMD to other parties, the restarting of plutonium program, and

the coming to fruition of the uranium enrichment program? All are actions being

undertaken by an unpredictable state that maintains a "level of paranoia, overheated

rhetoric, which is the results of three generations of Stalinist indoctrination" (Carter 2002,

13).

Imminence

If the primary objective of the North Korean Leadership is to stay in power and maintain the benefits that remaining in power accords, then it corresponds that they will take any action, make any threat, which will ensure that objective is met (Carter 2002, 11). It then follows that any threat of regime change will result in the use of any tool, to include nuclear, by the North Korean Leadership to prevent such loss of power. In fact, one of the tasks in OPLAN 5027, the numerical designator for the operations plan designed to counter a conventional attack on South Korea by North Korea, "reportedly involves a strategy of maneuver warfare north of the Demilitarized Zone with a goal of terminating the North Korean Regime, rather than simply terminating the war by returning North Korean forces to the Truce Line" (OPLAN 5027 2005, 3). Under such conditions, the North Koreans claim to have developed "nuclear deterrents" to prevent just such a result (Manyin, et al. 2005, CRS-36). It stands to reason then, that if a North Korean conventional attack into South Korea fails to achieve its objectives and the allied forces counterattack into North Korea, then the North Koreans will use WMD. In its planning assumptions, the United States believes it will have from three to ten days unambiguous warning prior to a conventional attack (OPLAN 5027 2005, 4). This strategic warning would consist of troop deployments, reserve call-ups, ammunition transfers and the occupation of attack positions along the border. Collateral to this option, keeping in mind that the enemy always gets a vote, is that if the North Koreans perceive an imminent attack the same assumption would exist that they would engage allied forces with WMD. Even assuming that the Allied Air Forces will be targeting known and suspected WMD sites from the first hours of the war, it is possible that some sites will not

94

be addressed and North Korea will maintain the capability to affect the battle with stocks of WMD.

Determining the imminence of a transfer of technology, the resumption of their plutonium program, or the readiness to build a uranium-based bomb is more problematic, reminiscent of the Israeli raid on Osirak in 1981. Three factors must be examined. First are the recent revelations of North Koreas collaboration with Pakistan in their nuclear program. Second is the transfer of missile technology that enables the development of delivery platforms. Finally, North Korea has established a pattern of agreeing to stop its nuclear weapons programs, only to later renege in order to receive additional inducements or to be caught in flagrant violation of their NPT commitments and agreements with the United States. The transfer of technology to another state is already accomplished; North Korea has already received nuclear technology from Khan Research Laboratories, apparently without the knowledge of the Pakistani authorities (Squassoni 2003, CRS-7). Upon senatorial questioning about the Pakistan-North Korean link, Deputy Secretary of State Richard Armitage stated, "We know it's both ways and we know a good bit about a North Korean-Pakistan relationship" (Squassoni 2003, CRS-7). Tied in with missile technology, the relationship may have begun "around 1997, when Pakistan first began receiving missile from North Korea" (Squassoni 2003, CRS-7). The acquisition of these missiles allowed Pakistan to develop the Ghauri-1 missile and "significantly increase Pakistan's ability to target India and improve Pakistan's ability to deploy nuclear warheads by increasing the payload" (Squassoni 2003, CRS-9). In 2002, a North Korean ship was intercepted in the Gulf of Aden "carrying 15 complete Scud missile bodies, 15 highly-explosive conventional warheads, and nitric acid headed for

Yemen" (Manyin et al. 2005, CRS-16). The ship was allowed to proceed because of Yemen's commitment to the war on terror (Squassoni 2003, CRS-13n). North Korea has also passed missile technology to Iran, "The Iranian Shahab-3 ballistic missile . . . is a North Korean Missile. The North Koreans call it a No-dong. Same thing" (Carter 2002, 8). In reaction to North Korea's established pattern of exporting missile technology and continuing nuclear weapons program, the United States has engaged other nations on "new agreements to search planes and ships carrying suspect cargo and to seize illegal weapons or missile technologies" (O'Hanlon and Levi 2003, 2). Under the Proliferation Security Initiative (PSI), The United States held a conference "with ten other countries . . . focusing on inspecting suspect North Korean ships in the participants' territorial waters" (O'Hanlon and Levi 2003, 2). Clearly, in regards to proliferation of WMD technology, North Korea is beyond the imminent stage.

In addition to the export of missiles and persistent development of nuclear weapons, North Korea has also conducted acts of terrorism against South Korea. In the 70s and 80s, North Korea conducted operations aimed at the assassination of South Koreas President and the embarrassment of South Korea. Three attempts, in 1970, 1974, and 1984 miscarried but the second attempt resulted in the death of the President's wife. In 1987, North Korean agents bombed a jetliner in an attempt to embarrass South Korea prior to the 1988 Seoul Olympics. The attack resulted in the deaths of 135 people on board (GlobalSecurity.org, North Korea-South Korea Tensions 2005). North Korea has demonstrated in full measure the capability, means, and willingness to use terrorism to achieve their ends. Combined with a known missile capability and the potential to develop weapons of mass destruction, North Korea capacity for terrorism presents a significant capacity to threaten the international community.

No Viable Alternatives

Currently the United States is maintaining viable alternatives in addressing North Korea, to include a military option. However, its primary position has been and continues to be the peaceful denuclearization of the Korean peninsula through diplomatic means. During the cold war, the United States was reluctant to engage North Korea in direct talks because of "the character of the Government under Kim Il Sung and the legacy of the Korean War" (*Chronology* 2005, 1). However in 1988, the United States engaged in discussions with North Korea and offered inducements, such as normalization of relations, if North Korea adhered to the NPT it had signed in 1985 (*Chronology* 2005, 1). By 1991, the United States had reportedly withdrawn "all nuclear weapons from South Korea" to reduce North Korea's "rationale for refusing to allow international inspection of its facilities" (Cronin 1994, 5). By 1994 the United States and North Korea had signed an agreed framework for discussions, in which the United States, Japan, and South Korea provided energy support and North Korea agreed to halt its development of nuclear facilities. In 1999, the Secretary of Defense visited "to convince Pyongyang to abandon its nuclear and missile development programs in exchange for improved diplomatic and economic relations" (*Chronology* 2005, 6). A year later in 2000, economic sanctions, in place since the Korean War, were eased by the Clinton administration and the United States Secretary of State visit North Korea to discuss their missile program (Manyin et al. 2005, CRS-10). Despite the Bush Administrations statement in 2002 that North Korea was in material breach of the Agreed Framework, the United States was willing to continue negotiations as long as they were multi-lateral (Hayes 2002, 1). By drawing China and Russia into the discussions, more effective pressure could be brought to bear on North Korea to halt their weapons development programs.

There is, however, a military option available and one that was looked at in 1994, prior to the signing of the Agreed Framework. The Clinton Administration looked at a military strike on the Yongbyon research reactor, in response to the removal of fuel rods containing "five or six bombs' worth of weapons-grade plutonium" (Carter 2003, 1). The strike was designed to "destroy the reactor, entomb the plutonium and that we [the US] could mount such a strike and carry it out without causing the reactor to create a Chernobyl-like radiological plume downwind" (Carter 2003, 1). Anticipating an attack by North Korea in reaction, the Secretary of Defense briefed the President on a plan to reinforce the Peninsula in an effort to "dramatically reduce the casualties" (Frontline: Kim's Nuclear Gamble 2005a, 3). The United States military creates and maintains contingency plans "as a 'last choice' if multilateral diplomacy fails to persuade North Korea to abandon its nuclear program" (Manyin et al. 2005, CRS-21). See figure 8.

Currently, the United States is currently pursuing options other than military to deal with North Korea. It has met success in expanding the negotiations to include South Korea, Japan, China and Russia, despite initial objections by North Korea, who demanded two-party talks with the United States. The "no viable options" also applies to North Korea, who must keep Russia and especially their major trading partner China from abandoning them during the negotiations. In short, "all reasonable alternatives" have not yet been exhausted.

Figure 8.   North Korea

Source: CIA, *Fact Book*, 2005, available from http://www.cia.gov/cia/publications/
factbook/geos/kn.html; Internet; accessed on 10 May 2005.

Proportionality

North Korea is a hard shell covering a rotten middle; however that does not mean

that the state would necessarily collapse when pressed, either militarily or diplomatically

(Frontline: Kim's Nuclear Gamble 2005b, 13). That hard shell consists of "a million men

on the DMZ." Thousands of artillery tubes are trained on Seoul, and SCUD missiles are

trained on South Korea (Carter 2002, 2). Despite famine, repression, and predictions

based on conventional wisdom, the North Korean state has demonstrated "amazing

staying power" (Frontline: Kim's Nuclear Gamble 2005b, 14). In Iraq, some of the

people living can remember a better time, before Saddam. In North Korea, three

generations have lived under the repression and indoctrination of a communist government and before that for those still living it was Japanese repression. In modern memory, what do the North Korean people know besides repression? As a result if either a preemptive or conventional attack, either offensive or a counterattack, is conducted the North Koreans can be expected to react disproportionately. In 1994, just such a preemptive attack was considered by the Clinton administration on the Yongbyon nuclear facility "but concludes that the consequences--an estimated 100,000 casualties from a North Korean reprisal are too severe" (*Chronology* 2005, 2). A precision attack itself would have been proportionate and precision in nature but the consequences would not have been. In anticipation of a conventional and overwhelming military response by North Korea, then Secretary of Defense Perry briefed the President on a troop reinforcement of the Korean peninsula (Frontline: Kim's Nuclear Gamble 2005b, 3). This is confirmed by "North Korean radio reports that Kim Jong-Il has warned that 'nuclear war could break out if the United States attacks his country's nuclear program'" (Manyin et al. 2005, CRS-21). The current concept of intercepting and inspecting North Korean ships, primarily for state-sponsored drug running, in territorial waters has promise of proportionality right up until it becomes the enforcement of undeclared sanctions. In 1994, North Korea shrilly proclaimed that it would "regard sanctions as a declaration of war" (Cronin 1994, 23). In view of the decline of the North Korean economy since then, this statement becomes more ominous. In short, if the United States takes any military action against the North Korean State, it must be prepared an all-out war to effect regime change. The key requirement in this preparation is international legitimacy.

Legitimacy

Obviously, the legitimacy of any preemptive military action is tied directly to the interests of the nations involved in the situation. For the United States to deal with North Korea and "be successful, any American strategy in that part of the world has to have some consensus with at least our allies, the South Koreans and the Japanese" (Carter 2002, 7). In demanding multiparty talks, the Bush administration recognized that, at least in this situation, China will either be the de facto ally of the United States or its de facto enemy (*Chronology* 2005, 9). China and South Korea stand to lose the most, aside from North Korea of course, as a result of any instability on the Korean peninsula. China from an increase in refugees and the loss of face caused by the intervention of a foreign power in what it considers to be its zone of influence, and South Korea, also because of refugees, but more importantly because they will be the immediate recipient of any North Korean retaliation. The inclusion of Russia, a long time ally and supporter of the North Korean regime, further accentuates not only the legitimacy of actions taken but also the bargaining power in negotiations with North Korea (Carter 2002, 10). The downside of bringing in additional parties to a negotiation is that these parties bring their own interests that do not always coincide with the desires of United States Foreign policy and often will actually conflict. Just as with Iraq, there are members of the Bush Administration that advocate "an overall strategy of isolating North Korea diplomatically and economically" with the "expressed hope and/or expectations of a collapse of the North Korean regime" (Manyin et al. 2005, CRS-4). As a result, "The United States did not put forward a detailed negotiating proposal until June 2004, despite requests from Chinese, Japanese, and South Korean Leaders (Manyin et al. 2005, CRS-4). Regime collapse has significant repercussions on China and South Korea, two nation's necessary to any

United States policy because they can place direct pressure on North Korea to adhere to

prior treaties and the negotiation process. Discussion of regime change also hinders allied

coordination and achievement of policy goals because, "As long as the regime itself is

questioned due to the North Korean nuclear issue, these countries that do not want it to

collapse, like China and South Korea, and those countries and individuals that think

regime change is necessary will not be able to coordinate" (Manyin et al. 2005, CRS-52).

The attitude of Russia and China in these negotiations are critical because they are

permanent members of the Security Council, having used the veto power to protect North

Korea from sanctions and other adverse actions in the past (Manyin et al. 2005, CRS-23).

In fact, a balance of power in the negotiations has been created requiring consensus in

which many "analysts used a 1-3-2" formulation to describe the dynamics of the six-party

talks; North Korea on its own; South Korea, Russia, and China favoring a more

conciliatory approach of offering incentives to North Korea and more emphasis on a

nuclear freeze instead of dismantlement; and Japan and the United States preferring a mix

of dialogue and pressure on Pyongyang (Manyin et al. 2005, CRS-5). However, both

Russia and China have called "on North Korea to "denuclearize" and for a normalization

of relations between Pyongyang and Washington 'on the basis of continued observation

of earlier reached agreements'" (Manyin et al. 2005, CRS-15). China has used its

influence both directly and indirectly to put pressure on North Korea to accede to

negotiations and adhere to previous commitments. In March 2003, "China reportedly

shuts down an oil pipeline to North Korea for three days. Some news reports say the

shutdown occurred after North Korea test-fired a cruise missile into the Sea of Japan on

March 10" (Manyin et al. 2005, CRS-21). And later in July of that same year, China ups

the pressure on North Korea to join multilateral talks to end the nuclear standoff during a

visit to Pyongyang by a special envoy from Beijing (CNN.com 2004, 3). China,

concerned with losing face in the international community, seems to be wearying of

North Korean intransigence and its affect on their status as a "rising economic and

political power" (Takahasi 2005, 1). Significantly impacting North Korea's bargaining

position,

> Zhang Liangui, a professor at the Central Party School of the Chinese Communist
> Party and a well-known commentator on Korean Peninsula issues, forcefully
> argued in a recent World Affairs magazine that if the current North Korean
> stalemate is not settled by July, the issue could be brought to the UN Security
> Council by October, Then, Zhang said, within the following month the council
> could decide to impose economic sanctions against North Korea, *including a
> naval blockade* [emphasis mine] by the UN-authorized coalition forces.
> (Takahashi 2005, 4)

In fact, due to the state of the North Korean economy, any sanctions, which

generally slow to take affect anyway, would be prolonged (Cronin 1994, 12). In terms of

the legitimacy of a preemptive strike on North Korea, it is significant that the People's

Republic of China, their main benefactor and main trading partner, is using such strong

language to encourage North Korean cooperation because a "naval blockade" carries with

it the power to forcibly stop any vessel attempting to violate the terms of the blockade. In

fact, execution of the current PSI could be extended to international waters and not just

the territorial waters of participating states. Active Chinese support for a blockade or

quarantine of North Korean ports, such as that imposed on Iraq by the United Nations in

1990, would be an essential prerequisite "to halt all inward and outward maritime

shipping in order to inspect and verify their cargoes and destinations" (Robertson 1991,

10). Inclusion of the People's Republic of China would significantly increase the effectiveness of PSI by closing Chinese ports to contraband items destined for North

Korea. The current evaluation of criterion established for a United States preemptive

strike on North Korea is depicted in table 7.

Table 7.   Analysis of a Preemptive Strike on North Korea

		Self Defense – "Caroline Case" Webster				
Conflict	NSS Applicability	Imminence of Attack		No Viable Alternatives	Proportionality	Legitimacy
		Immediacy	Schmitt's "Last Window of Opportunity"			
2003 US invasion of Iraq	Conventional Warfare			Met	Met	
North Korea	Nexus of WMD and Terrorism	Partially Met		Met	Partially Met	
Iran	Terrorism					

 Conditions for Criteria Met

 Conditions for Criteria Partially Met

Iran

Background

What would be the effect of the United States declaring a state of National

Emergency due to an "unusual and extraordinary threat to National Security" posed by

the "actions and policies of the Government of Iran?" Would people fill the streets protesting an administration bent on yet another conflict in the Middle East? Yet the United States has been in a declared state of emergency since 1995, declared by President Clinton due to Iran's "support for international terrorism, efforts to undermine the Middle East Peace process, and acquisition of weapons of mass destruction and the means to deliver them" (U.S. President 2005). On 10 March 2005, President Bush continued this national emergency for another year until 15 March 2006 because the administration determined Iran to be a continuing threat to national security (U.S. President 2005). In fact, since the 1979 Iranian Revolution and the seizure of 52 Americans for 444 days relations between the two countries has never been good (Yaphe 2002, 1).

Since 1979, Iran has tried to gain influence through out the region by exporting their version of theological revolution (Yaphe 2002, 1). As a result, they have developed into" the poster child for the nexus of terrorism and WMD" (Sokoloski and Clawson 2004, v). It is this crossroads or link between a rogue state and international terror that President Bush refers to as the "gravest danger our Nation faces" (U.S. President 2002, II-ii).

Despite the 1980 Algiers agreement that called for non-interference in Iran by the United States, Iran has been involved in some of the most deadly terrorist strikes against the United States. In 1983, Hezbollah terrorists with Iranian help blew up a United States Marine Corps Headquarters in Beirut, killing 241 United States Servicemen and forcing the United States to leave Lebanon (Sokoloski and Clawson 2004, v). In 1996, terrorists who were trained in Iran by Iranians blew up the Khobar Towers, a barracks facility used by United States Servicemen in Dharan, Saudi Arabia killing nineteen United States service members (Frontline: Terror and Tehran 2005e, 5-6). Because of these actions and support for terrorists groups elsewhere, the "state department has identified Iran as a state sponsor of terrorism since 1984" (Sokoloski and Clawson 2004, 83). Between support for terrorists, the takeover of the United States Embassy in Tehran, and the subsequent debacle of a rescue attempt, it is small wonder that the "American people appear to view Iran as a hostile country and support the U.S. military role in countering Iranian aggression" (Carus 1997, 5).

For the Iranians, the enmity of the United States has had a tremendous impact on both their economy and foreign policy. It was the United States that overthrew the government of Prime Minister Mossadegh in 1953 and installed the first "brutal un-Islamic" Shah (Sullivan 2002, 183). In 1982, less than two years after the end of the hostage crisis, when it looked like the Iranians might defeat Saddam Hussein and "pose a major strategic threat to the region," the United States began "a distinct 'tilt' towards Iraq" (Sokoloski and Clawson 2004, 102). This ensured a deeper isolation of Iran in the international community. Even when, Iraq used chemical weapons against Iran, there were only "nominal international protests" (Sokoloski and Clawson 2004, 103). In 1988, the USS Vincennes shot down an Iranian airliner killing all 290 persons on board (Stoessinger 2001, 192). That was bad enough, but the Iranians "were livid when they heard the commanding officer" was later promoted (Sullivan 2002, 186). As a result the United States is officially Iran's "greatest enemy, but at the same time many Iranians see the United States as the Promised Land" (Sokoloski and Clawson 2004, 83). Rule by Ayatollah has "wrecked" the Iranian economy resulting in 25 percent unemployment (Sokoloski and Clawson 2004, 9). Many young people "under 30 and with no memory of the 1979 revolution," are reacting by demonstrating against the government (Sokoloski and Clawson 2004, 83). Resentments, however, remain and in fact "the former US embassy in Tehran is now an anti-American museum" (Sullivan 2002, 183). Fortunately for the government, the United States is available as a ready-made enemy to draw the Iranian people's focus away from internal social and political problems against an "external threat" (Sokoloski and Clawson 2004, 8).

The government of Iran may hate the United States but they "fear encirclement" even more (Yaphe 2002, 3). The United States now operates or has influence in Afghanistan, Pakistan, Iraq, and Kuwait and throughout the GCC countries. As a result, the Iranians have concluded that in order to prevent further isolation and "compensate for military weakness," that they have to have a nuclear weapon for deterrent purposes, and principally, deterrence against the United States" (Pollack et al. 2005). Militarily weak compared to the United States, nuclear weapons give Iran the ability to effectively strike at what they believe to be the American center of gravity, "U.S. public opinion" (Desutter 1997, 4). Despite United States pressure and with the help of Russia, the Iranians are building a nuclear power plant on the Persian Gulf at Bushehr, which "like any uranium-fueled power reactor, would produce militarily significant amounts of plutonium in its fuel during operation" (Sokoloski and Clawson 2004, 23). In August 2002, an opposition group revealed, "that Iran is also building a heavy water plant at Arak" (Sokoloski and Clawson 2004, 23). Heavy water is used to "moderate the nuclear chain reaction in one type of nuclear reactor, that could be used either for civilian power production or to produce bomb materials. Bushehr does not use heavy water" and research reactors do not use heavy water in the amounts that Iran would be capable of producing (GlobalSecurity.org, Arak 2005, 1-2). Additionally, the IAEA has discovered that "Iran has a substantial uranium enrichment program" (Sokoloski and Clawson 2004, 23). When

the atomic nucleus of U-235 "is hit by a stray neutron, the atom will split and release

several other neutrons. If the percentage of the fissile isotopes is high enough, a self-

sustaining nuclear chain reaction will occur. To make weapons-grade uranium, a complex

enrichment process is required to raise the percentage of U-235 to around 90%"

(Frontline 2005, 1). Highly enriched uranium produces a bigger explosion than weapons

made of lower enriched uranium, less than 20 percent, or natural uranium where "only a

fraction of a percent of all uranium is U-235" (Frontline 2005, 1). A signatory of the

Nuclear Non-Proliferation Treaty (NPT), Iran has not complied with IAEA resolutions to

"come totally clean on its nuclear past" (Sokoloski and Clawson 2004, 9). See figure 9.

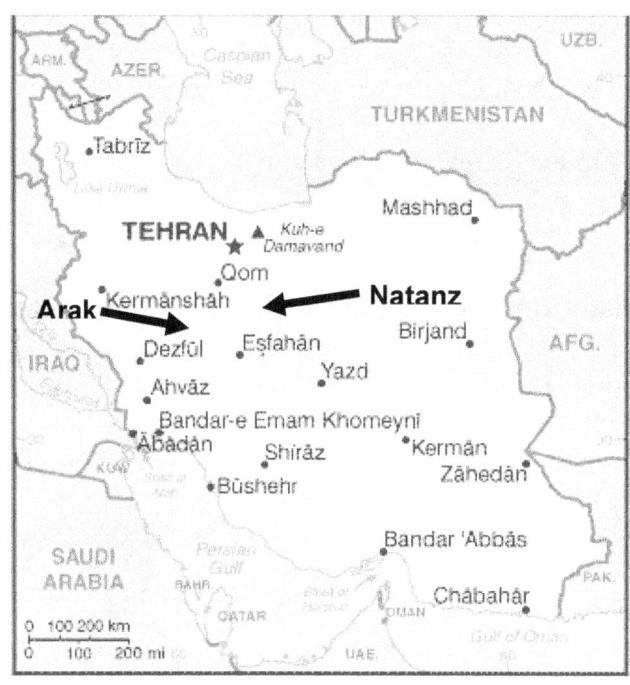

Figure 9.   Iran

Source: CIA, *Fact Book*, 2005, available from http://www.cia.gov/cia/publications/
factbook/geos/ir.html; Internet; accessed on 10 May 2005.

In 1991, despite their intransigence on nuclear development and support for terrorism, the Iranians made a "strategic decision to help the coalition by not interfering" (Sokoloski and Clawson 2004, 104). Again, in the 2001 invasion of Afghanistan and the 2003 invasion of Iraq, Iran made no objection and even helped in humanitarian aid and promised to assist the United States in recovering pilots (Yaphe 2002, 2). In the first case, Iran resented no reward for their actions in 1991 and in the second, the United States suspects Iran of interfering in Iraq (Sullivan 2002, 186). Despite this, Iran remains isolated and "at odds with the European Union (EU) over human rights; the IAEA for dodging agency resolutions that t come totally clean on its nuclear past; and the United States and most of the world for harboring terrorists-now including Al Qaeda agents-who are all too willing to use any means (including chemical, biological, or nuclear devices) to attack Israel, Europe, and the United States" (Sokoloski and Clawson 2004, 9).

Imminence

Much like the Israelis in the 1981 raid on Osirak, the United States faces a huge dilemma with the building of the nuclear power plant at Bushehr. Russia, playing the part of France in 1981, has assured the United States that Bushehr will not be used to produce fissile materials, even to the point of offering to buy back spent fuel rods from Iran (Sokoloski and Clawson 2004, 28). The United States, playing the part of Israel in 1981, based on its own intelligence information and Iran's history of enmity has significantly less confidence in Iranian good intentions. Also like Israel in 1981, the United States is faced with Schmitt's question of last window of opportunity. Should the United States conduct a preemptive strike on Bushehr before it goes into operation, thereby limiting collateral damage caused by inadvertently released radiation, or wait until intelligence

109

indicates that the Iranians are nearing completion of a nuclear weapon? In this regard, imminence is determined by the fact that "12-15 months after the reactor (Bushehr) goes into operation, it will contain roughly 60 bombs' worth of near weapons-grade plutonium" (Sokoloski and Clawson 2004, 15). Near-weapons grade bombs are not as powerful but still the "mean yield would be about 10 kilotons and the probability of exceeding a yield of about 20 kilotons would be about one-third, more or less than the yield of the bombs dropped on Japan (Sokoloski and Clawson 2004, 30). One-third the devastation of Hiroshima or Nagasaki is still a frightening vision for the future. For now this vision affects the United States' friends and allies in the region, because the Iranian Shahab-3 missile can only reach out to 1200-kilometers to hit targets in Turkey, Israel, Iraq, and the Persian Gulf within its reach (Yaphe 2002, 6n). Significantly, "the United States will face an ICBM threat from Iran by 2015, and Iran's missile inventory already is among the largest in the Middle East" (Sokoloski and Clawson 2004, 95). In 1996, Iran acquired SU-24s, which are "capable of delivering nuclear weapons" (MILNET 2004, 3). The IAEA Chairman, Mohammed El Baradei, has reported to the United Nations that Iran "may already have all the ingredients to test a nuclear weapon. Traces of weapons grade material continue to be found and the possible sites for weapons grade material manufacture continue to be overly busy" (MILNET 2004, 4). "Sources which wish to remain anonymous are split 50-50 on whether the device is actually ready for the test" (MILNET 2004, 5). In a sort of reverse "1967 Strait of Tiran" scenario, the combination of medium range missiles, nuclear delivery capable aircraft, and nuclear weapons means that Iran can close the Strait of Hormuz and hold the one-sixth world's oil supply hostage (Carus 1997, 3). More importantly for the United States, the closure of the "Strait while

110

threatening [Nuclear, Biological, and Chemical] NBC use could fulfill the threat stated by the head of the [Iranian Revolutionary Guard Corps] IRGC, General Rezai, to take 'at least 20,000 American forces' captive" (Desutter 1997, 4). In short, Iran already possesses the conventional-delivery capability to threaten nations in the region, the United States Forces deployed there, and, within ten years, will have the capability to directly threaten the United States homeland with Inter-Continental Ballistic Missiles.

To the United States, however, it is the documented link with international terrorism that provides the most imminent threat to the homeland. "Iran and the IRGC in particular, appear to have pursued a number of options for employing NBC weapons to attain or further its interests. These include a terrorist attack in which both the means of death and source of the attack are ambiguous" (Desutter 1997, 4). Iran has been identified as supporting several terrorist groups that "have shown a strong and abiding interest in WMD" including Hamas and the Palestinian Islamic Jihad (PIJ) (Committee on International Relations 2004, 3). The extent of support Iran is prepared to give is unknown, however, just nine months after 11 September, "a group of diplomats associated with the Iranian delegation to the UN were caught videotaping sites in New York during June 2002. They were asked to leave the US" (Sullivan 2002, 182). The United States is concerned even more with links between Iran and Al-Qaida, proposing "that Al Qaeda fugitives may have slipped into Iran, and that some may have found sanctuary there, including Abu Musaab Zarqawi" (Frontline: Terror and Tehran 2005e, 5). Control of these terrorist organizations would provide Iran with an unconventional nuclear (and chemical and biological) delivery method and "within weeks of being able to have a large arsenal of nuclear weapons, it will feel only more confident in sheltering

111

and supporting terrorists. Iran could use these groups as strategic proxies to pose the very nuclear threats . . . that Iran's own acquisition of a weapons option would otherwise accomplish" (Sokoloski and Clawson 2004, 18). For Al-Qaeda at least, the provision of NBC weapons by Iran would accomplish a goal that they have "extensively pursued" and significantly increase their influence in the world (Committee on International Relations 2004, 3).

What makes the current situation particularly dangerous is the effect of the significant United States military presence in the nations on either side of Iran, Iraq and Afghanistan, in addition to its usual naval presence in the Persian Gulf. Surrounded by United States bases from which preemptive attacks could be launched, "Iran's Defense Minister (Ali Shamkani) has expressed the government's deep disquiet at having American troops in Iraq and Afghanistan and hinted that some Iranian generals believe they should strike first if they sense an imminent threat from the United States" (Iran hints at pre-emption over threat from U.S. [2004]). Shamkani has openly stated, "Iran might launch preemptive strikes to protect its nuclear facilities if they are threatened" (Reuters 2004). Shamkani aimed this statement at both the United States and Israel, because Israel's policy, as with Iraq in 1981, is that "it will not allow Iran to build a nuclear weapon" (Iran hints at pre-emption over threat from U.S. [2004]). Finally, the Mullahs in Iran believe that a threat to them is a threat to Islam and there "are few apparent moral or religious impediments should Iranian leaders choose to employ NBC weapons (Desutter 1997, 1).

No Viable Alternatives

Currently the United States has at least two viable alternatives to a preemptive attack in order to achieve its objectives in regards to Iran. They are the pursuit of international pressure, through the European Union (EU) and the United Nations, and subversion of the current theocratic Iranian government. Both are currently ongoing and present necessary preconditions for the third alternative of preemption.

Based on current relations between the United States and Iran, the United States is supporting the current efforts of the United Kingdom, France, and Germany (EU-3) in negotiations with Iran in regards to the peaceful uses of nuclear energy and the implementation of the NPT. On 21 October 2003, an understanding was reached between the EU-3 and Iran, which "officials in Europe, Asia, Russia and China . . . see . . . as the first step to a larger deal" (Sokoloski and Clawson 2004, 7). Both Russia and China are the primary suppliers of both nuclear technology and equipment to Iran. To be effective, any international agreement must have their willing and active support. The United Nations, through the IAEA, also placed pressure on Iran by publishing a negative report resulting in panic in Tehran and full cooperation for six months (Pollack et al. 2005). It was only after the Europeans assured Iran that no sanctions would be forthcoming, that Tehran reneged on cooperation (Pollack et al. 2005). The United States has had more success in pressuring Russia and the Ukraine to refrain from cooperating with Iran in construction of the Bushehr nuclear power plant (GlobalSecurity.org, Bushehr 2005, 2). This, however, has only delayed construction and not stopped it completely if the Iranians agree to IAEA requirements and the return of spent fuel to Russia (GlobalSecurity.org, Bushehr 2005, 4).

In fact the Director General of the IAEA has repeatedly said that that there is no evidence to suggest that Iran has misused of diverted its nuclear technologies for military purposes (Pollack et al. 2005). This clearly leaves the United States in the "bad cop" role in pressing for "punitive measures for continued irresponsible behavior" (Sokoloski and Clawson 2004, 9). The effectiveness of this approach is demonstrated by Iran's continued attempts to get around the international pressure by failing to report to the IAEA its nuclear progress. For example in 1991, Iran imported 1.8 tons of natural uranium and failed to report it to the IAEA (Sokoloski and Clawson 2004, 24). On the positive side, Iran has either provided direct assistance or at least refrained from taking action in both the 1991 Gulf War and the 2001 War with Afghanistan. In regards to the 1991 Gulf War, Iran chose to stay on the sidelines and not protest United States action or become a party to the war, but resented not being rewarded for their tacit support. In the war with Afghanistan, "Iran agreed to assist American pilots downed on Iranian soil and to allow transshipment of food and humanitarian aid supplies for afghan refugees in Northwestern Afghanistan" (Yaphe 2002, 2). The United States has also used the economic element of power by blocking "loans and other assistance from international organizations like the World Bank and the IMF" (Sullivan 2002, 284). Because of its strong economic and political base, the United States has multiple levers with which to put pressure on Iran through international agencies. However, despite international pressure inspections of Iranian facilities have found "Violations, reams of violations" (Pollack et al. 2005).

The United States has also attempted to negotiate directly with Iran, but has been rebuffed by the "hardliners" in the government who use the external threat of the United States to stay in power (Sullivan 2002, 190). The Iranian Government has two sides, an elected side of the President and the parliament, and an unelected side "run by the conservative mullahs--the intelligence and the military and security branches" (Frontline: Terror and Tehran 2005b, 10). The elected side represents the people of Iran; however, "the levers of real power when it comes to foreign affairs are in the office of the vilayet-I-faqi, commander and chief of the armed forces, and supreme leaders of the revolution, Ayatollah Khamenei" (Sullivan 2002, 188). In fact the elected Iranian President, Mohammed Khatami, "despite his legitimization through two elections, has not asserted his legitimate power, and does not exercise power over any of the key issues in the country (Pollack et al. 2005). As a result "prospects for fundamental reform, much less outright revolutionary change, in the Islamic Republic of Iran are minimal in the short- to medium-term" (Sokoloski and Clawson 2004, 39). However, the Iranian government does have some key weaknesses that can be exploited. The first is religious and goes to the very heart of their style of theocracy, in that to "the majority of Shiite thinkers . . . no mere mortal could unite temporal and religious authority in one office" (Sokoloski and Clawson 2004, 42). This means that the kind of government established by the Ayatollah Khomeini is anathema to the Shia sect of Islam and brings its legitimacy into doubt. High unemployment and religious restrictions have had an adverse affect on public opinion and there appears to be a "growing pro-Americanism amongst the youth in Iran" (Sullivan 2002, 178). This is not to say that the Iranians are not patriotic towards their country, just that there are fractures in their support for their current form of government. In fact, "nationalism is reemerging as a defining element of the Islamic Republic" (Yaphe 2002, 3) "In an August 2002 poll, 63 percent of respondents believe that freedom and economic opportunity can only come as a result of 'a fundamental change' in Iran's system of government," the "maximum support the regime gets is 15-19 percent" (Sokoloski and Clawson 2004, 64-65). Despite attempts by the government to limit exposure to outside ideas, western influence continues to pour into Iran through satellite TV and the internet. Los Angeles based, Iranian expatriate run, Farsi speaking satellite TV broadcasts have been responsible for anti-government protests within Iran (Sokoloski and Clawson 2004, 94). Iran even paid Cuba to "Cuba to jam alternative Iranian broadcasting from Los Angeles for fear of its seditious influence" (Sokoloski and Clawson 2004, 11). As a result, there are those that claim that "Iran's revolutionary government can be overthrown within two years should the United States adopt a more robust policy of empowering the Iranian people to change the regime in Tehran" (Sokoloski and Clawson 2004, 61).

Both options presented are also preferable from the military perspective because of the difficulty of being able to decisively destroy all potential Iranian WMD sites and weapons. Learning from the Iraqi experience in 1981, the Iranians have "dispersed" and hidden "its nuclear infrastructure" (Sokoloski and Clawson 2004, 113). "Iran's most important facilities are not at Bushehr . . . but scattered across the country, at clandestine sites, under military control. The clandestine sites are not 'declared'--that is they are not subject to I.A.E.A. inspection" (Frontline: Terror and Tehran 2005e, 4). As a result "locations of key facilities in . . . Iran remain unknown" (Perkovich 2003, 68).

Proportionality

As with North Korea, any strike on Iran could have potentially devastating consequences for the United States' allies and forces in the region. "Should it choose to retaliate, Iran has several options: it could disrupt oil shipments from the Persian Gulf, attack United States Naval assets in the region; or engage in subversion and terrorism

116

against United States Allies and interests" (Sokoloski and Clawson 2004, 124).

Disruption of one-sixths of the world's oil deliveries by closure of the Strait of Hormuz would have an enormous strategic effect on the legitimacy of any United States preemptive action. "Iran's navy . . . could stem the flow of oil from the Gulf for brief periods by employing a layered force of diesel-powered KILO submarines, missile patrol boats, naval mines, and sea and shore-based anti ship cruise missiles" (Sokoloski and Clawson 2004, 124). Additionally the closure would trap United States forces deployed to the region and limit, though not prevent additional deployments of forces. It would require a force of significant size to force the Strait open again and make them safe for commercial traffic. The current government of Iran is, at least rhetorically, vehemently anti-American and their "capacity for terror and subversion remains one of Tehran's few levers in the event of a confrontation with the United States (Sokoloski and Clawson 2004, 124). The element of government responsible for WMD development and employment is the IRGC, which "is well organized, coherent, and virulent in their hatred of the United States" (Desutter 1997, 1). Additionally, the control of the government over the IRGC is limited and they "might be capable of taking military action even without political or religious direction" (Desutter 1997, 3). In short, even a preemptive strike to destroy Bushehr might escalate into a regional conflict with the United States potentially branded as the aggressor. With conventional forces too weak to retaliate effectively, "NBC weapons offer Iran a counterbalance to the United States' overwhelming conventional superiority" (Desutter 1997, 2). So the possibility of Iranian use of WMD in the region to counter the United States or outside the region through terrorist action is high (Sokoloski and Clawson 2004, 114). Balancing this is the fact that even "with the

117

best planning, such a strike would be unlikely to destroy all of Iran's covert weapons efforts or stop its nuclear scientists from resuming work" (Sokoloski and Clawson 2004, 6). As mentioned earlier, key "elements of Iran's nuclear program are dispersed and concealed" (Sokoloski and Clawson 2004, 114). While it may be possible to "entomb" the reactors within their own debris by a military strike as planned for the reactor at Yongbyon in 1994, it is still "preferable to target these (Iranian reactors) prior to start-up to avoid exposing civilians downwind to fallout" (Sokoloski and Clawson 2004, 120). Also, just as the Israelis had to consider French workers in their attack plans, there are hundreds of Russian nuclear workers engaged in building the Bushehr reactor and training Iranian technicians to operate the facility (GlobalSecurity.org, Bushehr 2005). Finally, with the rise of nationalism in Iran any strike may cause the intensification of anti-American feeling and validation of the current government's policies towards the United States and "undermine" United States efforts to encourage "political change" and improve relations (Sokoloski and Clawson 2004, 114).

Legitimacy

Due to the failure, first to convince the world about and later to find, WMD in Iraq "tensions about the Iraq WMD issue still poison relations and weaken the ability of the U.S. to respond" (Sokoloski and Clawson 2004, vi). As a result, any intelligence regarding Iran's WMD use is suspect for either hard intelligence reasons or political ones. However, the "intelligence about the Iran threat is coming from a United Nations Agency-namely, the International Atomic Energy Agency-and there is no doubt that Iran is developing worrisome capabilities" (Sokoloski and Clawson 2004, vi). Worrisome enough "the IAEA Board of Governors (including Russia) to demand that Iran freeze its enrichment and possible reprocessing facilities, allow more intrusive inspections and clarify its past nuclear activities" (Sokoloski and Clawson 2004, 12-13). "The advanced status of the Iranian nuclear program has been revealed most explicitly in recent visits to the country buy IAEA inspectors . . . the Europeans, Russians, and Japanese, now seem to share American concerns about what the Iranians are up to" (Sokoloski and Clawson 2004, 111). For Iran, somewhat of an isolated pariah nation, close ties to China and Russia are dictated more by their desire to limit United States influence than to help Iran in any meaningful manner (Sokoloski and Clawson 2004, 9). In 2001, Russia signed a military accord with Iran that could mean over 300 million dollars worth of arms sales (Frontline: Terror and Tehran 2005d, 12). However, Russia itself seems to be getting increasingly cold feet over the specter of Iranian nuclear weapons but is locked into a deal that it cannot extricate itself without losing face and appearing to succumb to United States pressure (Katz 2004, 1).

The United States policy towards Iran is one of economic and political pressure, however, always in the background is the military option. According to the United States National Security Advisor, "We've now got a strategic agenda with the Europeans, and we've also got agreements from the Europeans that if their negotiations do not succeed and Iran resumes its effort to move toward a nuclear capability, then we will go together and take it to the United Nations" (Associated Press 2005, 1-2). The United States is backing the effort of the EU to negotiate a peaceful solution to the Iranian nuclear threat but remains in the role of the bad cop. This is what the United States attempted to accomplish during the Iraq crisis in 2003 but could not get the Europeans, or China for that matter, to agree to a second resolution because a perceived rush to war. The basic

119

flaw in the argument on engaging Iran, however, is whether they will abide by their agreements. Iran has acceded to the NPT however, the "basic deal behind the Treaty on the Non-Proliferation of Nuclear Weapons (NPT) is that countries are allowed to acquire a wide range of troubling capabilities in return for being open and transparent" (Sokoloski and Clawson 2004, vii). If then the Iranians are allowed to acquire materials for peaceful nuclear energy production which can also be used for weapons development then, as IAEA Director General El Baradei pointed out, "There is no monitoring effort, he (IAEA Director General El Baradei) explained, not even the additional protocol the IAEA is asking Iran to implement, that can prevent nations from acquiring nuclear weapons sol long as they are allowed to have enrichment, reprocessing, and power reactor programs" (Sokoloski and Clawson 2004, 15).

At this point, it becomes a gentlemen's agreement, with few "gentlemen" involved. On 15 November 2004, Iran, the United Kingdom, France, and Germany signed an agreement in which Iran agreed not to pursue nuclear weapons and "full cooperation and transparency with the IAEA" and in return, the EU would "actively support the opening of Iranian accession negotiations at the WTO" (International Atomic Energy 2004, 3). In this matter, the Europeans are clearly in the role of the good cop, offering "significant incentives for responsible behavior" (Sokoloski and Clawson 2004, vi). Despite these overt promises, Iran's history of hiding facilities such as the Natanz underground uranium enrichment plant and the Arak heavy water plant continues to reduce confidence in Iran's faithful adherence to the multitude of agreements they have signed with the United Nations and the EU (Sokoloski and Clawson 2004, 23). Small wonder the United States publicly implies a military option to prevent the Iranians from

120

getting a bomb. The current evaluation of criterion established for a United States preemptive strike on Iran is depicted in table 8.

Table 8.   Analysis of a Preemptive Strike on Iran

Conflict	NSS Applicability	Self Defense – "Caroline Case" Webster				
		Imminence of Attack		No Viable Alternatives	Proportionality	Legitimacy
		Immediacy	Schmitt's "Last Window of Opportunity"			
2003 US invasion of Iraq	Conventional Warfare			Met	Met	
North Korea	Nexus of WMD and Terrorism	Met		Met	Partially Met	
Iran	Terrorism	Met	Partially Met	Partially Met	Partially Met	Partially Met

 Conditions for Criteria Met

 Conditions for Criteria Partially Met

Conclusion

On 4 July 1821, Secretary of State John Quincy Adams addressed the Congress of the United States about what differentiated the United States from the "old world." It was an idealistic view from a new country. One that looked to the international community as equals and, despite rebuffs, continued to offer the "honest hand of friendship" (Adams 1821). However, the United States was interested neither in dominating others nor in

121

subjugating her own interest to the reach for power that affected old Europe. Her only interest was in being the example of freedom and independence and not in using force to propel it. Using force to assist other countries to gain freedom and independence was a road that led to "wars of interest and intrigue" (Adams 1821). The United States would be the "champion and vindicator" of her own independence and freedom, "But she goes not abroad, in search of monsters to destroy" (Adams 1821).

Since then, the United States has gone abroad several hundred times in the guise of freedom's "champion and vindicator." In two world wars, a cold war, and a host of lesser conflicts and interventions, the United States has repeatedly sent her blood and treasure overseas to fight aggression and to defend her own interests. This earned the United States many friends and allies throughout the world, but it also made enemies. Times and circumstances have changed with the fall of the Soviet Union and rendered the old balance of power moot. The United States was now the superpower and had learned from the Second World War about the dangers of isolationism. Remaining safe behind the oceans was as dangerous a course of action as engaging the world. Those oceans would not keep the United States safe forever and 180 years after John Quincy Adams warned about destroying "monsters" abroad, monsters of another sort struck the United States at home destroying the World Trade Center, severely damaging the Pentagon, and killing almost 3,000 people.

The world had changed again and the Bush administration responded with the *NSS* of 2002 and the adoption of the doctrine of preemption. The terrorist attacks on 11 September demonstrated the threat posed by nonstate actors. Deterrence, a strategy that brought down the Union of Soviet Socialist Republics and its allies, would not work against enemies that owned no terrain, no manufacturing capability, and no population. What makes the terrorists especially dangerous is the potential to conduct an operation like 11 September using WMD. Like 11 September, there exists the possibility of little to no warning before the terrorists strike. Unlike 11 September, the use of even a near weapons grade plutonium bomb would be more widespread in its effects. The "mean yield [of a near weapons grade bomb] would be about 10 kilotons and the probability of exceeding a yield of about 20 kilotons would be about one-third, more or less the yield of the bombs dropped on Japan," (Sokoloski and Clawson 2004, 30). A report published by Lawrence Livermore in 1995 stated that even "reactor-grade (RG) plutonium . . . can be used to construct a nuclear weapon with a yield of 'at least a kiloton'" (Sokoloski and Clawson 2004, 30). In either case, the United States would be counting casualties in the millions, not the thousands. In order to break the chain, then, the nexus has to be broken at the source. That source is those states that harbor terrorists and provide the sanctuary, time, and money to develop weapons with which to attack the United States.

Precedent for preemptive and preventive strikes has been set in the international arena by a multitude of nations, however Israeli actions and the subsequent reactions of the international community most clearly demonstrates the impact of legitimacy on adopting a preemptive strategy. Israeli attempts to shape international support, or their failure to do so, prior to conducting strikes meant the difference between international protection and international isolation as a pariah state. On the one hand, Israel's active diplomatic efforts prior to the 1967 attack on Egypt ensured that the United States and the United Kingdom prevented their condemnation in the Security Council and the possible subsequent emplacement of sanctions, despite French antagonism and Soviet enmity. On

123

the other hand, Israel's deliberate decision not to even inform their closest ally, the United States, before conducting the 1981 raid on Osirak, and their Prime Minister's broken promise to the American President to stop at the 40-kilometer line in the 1982 invasion of Lebanon, directly resulted in condemnation in the Security Council and reinforced their status as a "pariah" state. In latter two case studies, the Israeli Government (on both occasions headed by Menachem Begin) utterly failed to shape the international landscape and are still paying the price in terror attacks and international isolation.

For the United States, the adoption of a preemptive strategy was directed primarily at the axis of evil that meant, and means, Iraq, North Korea, and Iran. Iraq was apparently the first test case of the new Bush strategy but, as has been demonstrated, it did not meet the criteria for preemption based Webster's enunciation. Though a tenuous cease-fire was in effect between Iraq and the coalition after the 1991 Persian Gulf War, a state of war still existed and no formal conclusion to the war in the form of a peace treaty had occurred. Between 1991 and 2003, Iraq repeatedly ignored or directly violated the conditions of the cease-fire resulting in numerous air attacks by the Coalition on Iraqi targets. The fact that Iraq clearly could not effectively threaten the United States, due to the degradation of its armed forces, did not mean that they could not threaten asymmetrically through terrorism linked with WMD. This was the case that Secretary of State Colin Powell attempted, and failed, to make before the United Nations Security Council in February 2003. In November 2002, he had succeeded in convincing the Security Council that Iraq was a threat, prompting the unanimous passage of UNSCR 1441 that declared Iraq "guilty of a material breach of its obligations." Secretary Powell,

124

however, was unable to convince the Security Council, specifically France and Russia, that Iraq was an imminent threat. The result was, for a time, a desperate lack of international support, specifically troops, infrastructure development support, and financial contributions.

Despite the Kim Jong-Il government's ties to terror groups, the case study of North Korea is more of a traditional state-on-state threat. The questionable stability, both psychologically and politically, of the North Korean government gives rise to serious concerns not only of the employment of nuclear weapons but also what happens to them if the government falls. North Korea, even more than Iraq ever was, is a direct and continuing threat to American interests in the region. So much so that a preemptive strike on Yongbyon nuclear power plant was briefed to the President in 1994. The recent claim by the Democratic People's Republic that it already has nuclear weapons means that the last window of opportunity has already closed. Their demonstrated capability to deliver those weapons against United States international interests in the region, specifically South Korea and Japan, also means that the threat is significantly higher now than it was in 1994. However, any use of nuclear weapons by North Korea would practically and geographically concern to both China and Russia very much. Bordering on the rogue state, and because of close historical and economic relations, China and Russia have great influence with the North Korean Government. It is in neither country's interest to have either North Korea fail or for the North Koreans to engage the United States in a war. That is the diplomatic reason for United States support of six-party talks vice bilateral communications with North Korea. It provides viable diplomatic, economic and informational alternatives to a military option. Six-party talks also place the onus on

Russia and China to keep the Democratic Peoples Republic of Korea (DPRK) in line and cooperating with the United Nations and the IAEA. If they fail, and Chinese patience with North Korean intransigence seems to be wearing thin, then that only enhances the legitimacy of and builds support for a preemptive strike on North Korea.

Iran's position is weaker and the United States' position is consequently proportionately stronger. Since 1979, they have pursued a political agenda highly colored by their theology, which is a break from traditional Shia philosophy. The Iranians initially promoted "Islamic revolution" in neighboring countries, alienating them from other states in the region and isolating their foreign policy to some degree. However, Iran does have the ability, through Medium Range Ballistic Missiles, links with terrorism, and a developing Inter-Continental Ballistic Missile capability to effectively strike at United States interests and allies not only in the Gulf region but also eventually in the United States homeland. However, the negotiations being conducted by the EU with Iran, demonstrated ability of the United States to put pressure on Russia, and the growing Iranian people's dissatisfaction with their government and the consequent rise of pro-American feelings among the youth give the United States several viable alternatives to oppose the Iranian government without resorting to military action. For each of these options there exist quantifiable measures of effectiveness. Iranian acceptance and implementation of negotiated agreements with the EU, the agreement to return the irradiated plutonium from the Bushehr nuclear facility to Russia, the reaction of the unelected part of the Iranian Government to the demands for reform from the elected portion under Khatami and the Iranian people are all indicators of whether Iran poses an increasing or decreasing imminent threat. The Iranian precedence for all of these

126

indicators is not good. The unelected leadership under Ayatollah Khameini has previously reneged on agreements with the EU, not yet agreed (or disagreed) to return plutonium to Russia, have marginalized the elected president, and imprisoned liberal activists. Bent on becoming a regional power, Iran has actually impeded its political influence within the region and, despite trading with both Russia and China, has no real close political ties with any of the five-permanent members of the Security Council. By failing in their obligations under the NPT and good faith negotiations with the EU and Russia, Iran, like North Korea, actually enhances the legitimacy of a preemptive strike by the United States.

There is a growing discussion on the concept of post-hoc legitimacy. Post-hoc legitimacy essentially means that a preemptive strike, which is not legitimate at the time of the incident, may gain legitimacy over time. This is the argument that is now used for the 1981 raid on Osirak. That the raid can now be determined to be legitimate, because it prevented Iraq from developing a nuclear weapon which it then would have been available for use against the coalition in 1991, thereby saving thousands of lives ad according legitimacy. A better argument is made for legitimizing NATO's attack on Serbia in defense of the Kossovars. The United Nations essentially conferred post-hoc legitimacy on NATO's operations by adopting favorable resolutions and material support. This argument is especially important in terms of the United State's invasion of Iraq because it opens the door for actions to be taken now in the belief that later evidence will exonerate the perpetrator. In Jomini's words, "It may be excused, if not approved, when induced by great interests or when conducted with good motives." For example, Israel and the United States conducted military attacks, in 1967 and 2003, respectively. As a result of victorious military action, Israel occupied the Golan Heights, the West Bank, and the Gaza Strip and refused to relinquish them because of their experience after returning territory from the 1956 War. In 1982, it was partly in response to pressure for elections in these occupied territories that Prime Minister Begin agreed to an invasion of Lebanon, calculating that a defeat of the PLO in Lebanon would influence these elections in a manner favorable to Israel. Instead, indefinite occupation reduced Israeli legitimacy and remained a rallying point for all of the anti-Israel nations and terrorist factions. The United States-led invasion of Iraq in 2003 and subsequent actions within the country, on the contrary, compares favorably to the Israeli experience. While not achieving legitimacy from the United Nations for the invasion, the subsequent movement of United Nations personnel and organizations into Iraq after "Major Combat Operations" had been completed may have accorded post-hoc legitimacy to the Coalition actions. In short, the United Nations may not have approved the method of regime removal, but it was not necessarily concerned over a ruthless dictator's plight. When faced with the fact that Iraq had to have a new government and international support if it was to be a viable state, the United Nations legitimized the overthrow de facto by accepting the current conditions and establishing a headquarters in Baghdad. In fact, there has been increasing acceptance of interventions to avert humanitarian catastrophe and this may have lowered the bar to military interventions in other areas, especially concerning WMD and terrorism. There is evidence that if the United States had found WMD in Iraq, or had the United States produced sufficient evidence, that there would have been significantly more European support for the initial invasion in 2003.

Finally, this brings to the question of legality. Two articles in different International treaties are pertinent. The first is Article 18 of the Charter of the International Court of Justice, which states that international law is not only based on treaties but also on international custom. The second is Article 51 of the United Nations Charter which states that the legitimate use of force can only be in self-defense or when authorized by the United Nations Security Council "to maintain or restore international peace and security." Legality then is not as cut and dried, as one would think if it is based on custom or the authorization of an international political body. The United States may have been able to shape successfully international opinion, for example, the five-permanent members, if it had not been in such a hurry. Consequently, many of the post-major combat operation difficulties, problems with acceptance by the Iraqi people and flow of international support, among other things, may have been avoided. With this in mind then, the only possible conclusion is that the United States may indeed be able to shape international opinion so that a preemptive attack is accepted as legitimate with the consequent availability of resources from the international community that legitimacy accords. However, because of the distrust accrued by the failure to gain legitimacy prior to the 2003 invasion and to achieve post-hoc legitimacy by the failure to find WMD in Iraq afterwards, the bar to gaining legitimacy in the future for preemptive attacks has been raised. Whether deliberate or not, the confusion of the terms preemptive versus preventive in the *NSS* of 2002 has come home to roost. In short, while shaping the international community may lower the bar to action, not shaping the international community definitely raises the bar that much higher for the United States in future operations. In the midst of the GWOT, the United States cannot afford to lose the strategic moral high ground for practical reasons. It provides freedom of maneuver and freedom of action for the United States Armed Forces to prevent another terrorist attack like that of 11 September.

ADDRESS TO CONGRESS BY SECRETARY OF STATE
JOHN QUINCY ADAMS, 4 JULY 1821

AND NOW, FRIENDS AND COUNTRYMEN, if the wise and learned philosophers of the elder world, the first observers of nutation and aberration, the discoverers of maddening ether and invisible planets, the inventors of Congreve rockets and Shrapnel shells, should find their hearts disposed to enquire what has America done for the benefit of mankind?

Let our answer be this: America, with the same voice which spoke herself into existence as a nation, proclaimed to mankind the inextinguishable rights of human nature, and the only lawful foundations of government. America, in the assembly of nations, since her admission among them, has invariably, though often fruitlessly, held forth to them the hand of honest friendship, of equal freedom, of generous reciprocity.

She has uniformly spoken among them, though often to heedless and often to disdainful ears, the language of equal liberty, of equal justice, and of equal rights.

She has, in the lapse of nearly half a century, without a single exception, respected the independence of other nations while asserting and maintaining her own.

She has abstained from interference in the concerns of others, even when conflict has been for principles to which she clings, as to the last vital drop that visits the heart.

She has seen that probably for centuries to come, all the contests of that Aceldama the European world, will be contests of inveterate power, and emerging right.

Wherever the standard of freedom and Independence has been or shall be unfurled, there will her heart, her benedictions and her prayers be.

But she goes not abroad, in search of monsters to destroy. [Emphasis mine]

She is the well-wisher to the freedom and independence of all.

She is the champion and vindicator only of her own.

She will commend the general cause by the countenance of her voice, and the benignant sympathy of her example.

She well knows that by once enlisting under other banners than her own, were they even the banners of foreign independence, she would involve herself beyond the power of extrication, in all the wars of interest and intrigue, of individual avarice, envy, and ambition, which assume the colors and usurp the standard of freedom.

The fundamental maxims of her policy would insensibly change from liberty to force.

She might become the dictatress of the world. She would be no longer the ruler of her own spirit.

[America's] glory is not dominion, but liberty. Her march is the march of the mind. She has a spear and a shield: but the motto upon her shield is, Freedom, Independence, Peace. This has been her Declaration: this has been, as far as her necessary intercourse with the rest of mankind would permit, her practice.

REFERENCE LIST

Abrams, Elliott, Richard L. Armitage, William J. Bennett, Jeffrey Bergner, John Bolton, Paula Dobriansky, Francis Fukuyama, Robert Kagan, Zalmay Khalilzard, William Kristol, Richard Perle, Peter W. Rodman, Donald Rumsfeld, William Schneider, Jr., Vin Weber, Paul Wolfowitz, R. James Woolsey, and Robert B. Zoellick. 1998. Letter to President Clinton on Iraq. Available from http://www.new americancentury.org/iraqclintonletter.htm. Internet. Accessed on 5 April 2005.

Adams, John Quincy. 1821. Warning against the search for monsters to destroy, 4 July. Available from http://www.fff.org/freedom/1001e.asp. Internet. Accessed on 25 March 2005.

Adelman, Howard. 2003. Law, ethics and preemption: The case of Iraq. A Paper for presentation at the Socratic Forum at Parliament House, Brisbane, Australia, 1 December, held under the auspices of the Key Centre for Ethics, Law, Justice, and Governance, Griffith University.

Associated Press. 2005. Hadley: Iran, don't get comfortable, 13 March. Available from http://www.foxnews.com/story/0,2933,150265,00.html. Internet. Accessed on 30 March 2005.

Baker, S. C. 2003. Operation Iraqi Freedom: An operational opportunity to complete the strategic objectives of Desert Storm. Research Project, Naval War College, Newport, RI.

Bavly, Dan, and Eliahu Salpeter. 1984. *Fire in Beirut, Israel's war in Lebanon with the PLO*. New York, NY: Stein and Day.

Beres, Louis René. 2004. International law is not a suicide pact. *Jewishpress.com*, 20 October. Available from http://thejewishpress.com/news_article_print.asp? article=472. Internet. Accessed on 6 December 2004.

Beres, Louis Rene, Dr., and Col. (IDF Res.) Yoash Tsiddon-Chatto. 1997. In support of anticipatory self-defense: Israel, Osiraq, and international law, June. Available from http://www.freeman.org/m_online/jun97/beres1.htm. Internet. Accessed on 16 October 2004.

Blaher, J. Andrew. 2004. Preemption: Making America more secure? Research Project, U.S. Army War College, Carlisle Barracks, PA.

Blix, Hans. 2003. An update on inspection to the UN security council by the executive chairman of UNMOVIC, 27 January. Available from http://www.un.org/depts/ unmovic/Bx27.htm. Internet. Accessed on 25 March 2005.

Brown, Herb, Mark L. Bowlin, and Scott C. Sheltz. 2002. How the Bush doctrine of preemptive strike meets the test of the Powell doctrine. Joint and Combined Staff Officers School, Joint Forces Staff College, Norfolk, VA.,

Bunn, M. Elaine. 2003. Preemptive doctrine: When, how and to what effect? *Strategic Forum* 200 (July): 1-8.

Butler, Richard, Executive Director of UNSCOM. Remarks to United Nations Security Council, January 1999. Available from http://www.ceip.org/programs/npp/butler 99.htm. Internet. Accessed on 25 March 2005.

California State University, Sacramento. 2004. *OBE 150 case study guide*. Available from http://www.csus.edu/indiv/e/estenson/CaseStudy_Guide.htm. Internet. Accessed on 17 October 2004.

Carnegie Endowment for International Peace. 2005. *Deadly arsenals*. Available from http://www.ceip.org/files/projects/npp/resources/DeadlyArsenals/chapters%20(P DF)/16-iraq.pdf. Internet. Accessed on 25 March 2005.

Carter, Ashton. 2003. Interview by Frontline on 3 March. Available from http://www. pbs.org/wgbh/pages/frontline/shows/kim/interviews/acarter.html. Internet. Accessed on 30 March 2005.

Carus, W. Seth. 1997. *Iran as a military threat*, Strategic Forum Number 113. Available from http://www.ndu.edu/inss/strforum/h6.html. Internet. Accessed on 9 April 2005.

Chronology. 2005. *See* Frontline: Kim's Nuclear Gamble. 2005a.

Cirincione, Joseph. 2003. Can preventive war cure proliferation? *Foreign Policy* (July/August): 66-69. Available from http://www.foreignpolicy.com/story/cms. php?story_id=131&print=1. Internet. Accessed on 20 October 2004.

Claire, Rodger W. 2004. *Raid on the sun*. New York: Broadway Books.

CNN.com. 2004. Timeline: North Korea's nuclear weapons development. Available from http://www.cnn.com/2003/WORLD/asiapcf/east/08/20/nkorea.timeline. nuclear. Internet. Accessed on 30 March 2005.

Crockett, James B. 2003. From anticipatory counterattack to anticipatory self-defense – the past, present, and future of preemption. Research Project, U.S. Army War College, Carlisle Barracks, PA.

Davis, M. Thomas. 1987. *40Km into Lebanon: Israel's 1982 invasion*. Washington, DC: National Defense University Press.

Dean, Jonathan, Chairman. United Nations Association. 2003. *Report of the task force on peace and security*. Washington, DC: Government Printing Office.

Declaration of Independence. Representatives of the United States. Available from http://www.usconstitution.net/declar.html. Internet. Accessed on 13 February, 2005

Desutter, Paula. 1997. *Deterring Iranian NBC use*, Strategic Forum Number 110, April. Available from http://www.ndu.edu/inss/strforum/SF110/forum110.html. Internet. Accessed on 9 April 2005.

Dinstein, Yoram. 2001. *War, aggression and self-defence*. 3rd ed. Cambridge, Great Britain: Cambridge University Press.

Director of Central Intelligence. 2002. *Iraq's weapons of mass destruction programs*, October. Available from http://www.cia.gov/cia/reports/iraq_wmd/iraq_oct_2002.htm. Internet. Accessed on 25 March 2005.

Dupuy, Trevor N. 1984. *Elusive victory: The Arab-Israeli wars, 1947-1974*. Fairfax, VA: Hero Books.

Dupuy, Trevor N., and Paul Martell. 1986. *Flawed victory, The Arab-Israeli conflict and the 1982 war in Lebanon*. Fairfax, VA: Hero Books.

European Union External Relations. 2002. *The EU's relations with the Democratic People's Republic of Korea-DPRK (North Korea)*. Available from http://europa.eu.int/comm/external_relations/north_korea/intro. Internet. Accessed on 30 March 2005.

Federation of American Scientists. 2004. *Osiraq / Tammuz I, 33°12'30"N 44°31'30"E.* Available from http://fas.org/nuke/guide/iraq/facility/osiraq.htm. Internet. Accessed on 23 September 2004.

Frontline. 2005. *Frequently asked questions*. Available from http://www.pbs.org/wgbh/pages/frontline/shows/nukes/stuff/faqs.html. Internet. Accessed on 11 April 2005.

Frontline: Kim's Nuclear Gamble. 2005a. *Chronology*. Available from http://www.pbs.org/wgbh/pages/frontline/shows/kim/etc/cron.html. Internet. Accessed on 30 March 2005.

_____. 2005b. *Examining the lessons of the 1994 US-North Korea deal*. Available from http://www.pbs.org/wgbh/pages/frontline/shows/kim/ themes/lessons.html. Internet. Accessed on 30 March 2005.

Frontline: Terror and Tehran. 2005a. *Analysis: Iran and the bomb*. Available from http://www.pbs.org/wgbh/pages/frontline/shows/tehran/axis/wmd.html. Internet. Accessed on 3 April 2005.

_____. 2005b. *Analysis: The long reach of a speech*. Available from http://www.pbs. org/ wgbh/pages/frontline/shows/tehran/axis/axis.html. Internet. Accessed on 3 April 2005.

_____. 2005c. *Analysis: Who's a terrorist?* Available from http://www.pbs.org/wgbh/ pages/frontline/shows/tehran/axis/terror.html. Internet. Accessed on 3 April 2005.

_____. 2005d. *Chronology-U.S.-Iran relations, 1906-2002*. Available from http://www.pbs.org/wgbh/pages/frontline/shows/tehran/etc/cron.html. Internet. Accessed on 3 April 2005.

_____. 2005e. *How Iran entered the axis*. Available from http://www.pbs.org/wgbh/ pages/frontline/shows/tehran/axis/map.html. Internet. Accessed on 3 April 2005.

Gaddis, John Lewis. 2004a. A grand strategy of transformation, *current strategic concepts syllabus/book of readings*. The US Army Command and General Staff College, Fort Leavenworth, Kansas.

_____. 2004b. *Surprise, security, and the American experience*. Cambridge, MA: Harvard University Press.

Gentile, Gian P. 2000. Planning for preventive war, 1945-1950. *Joint Forces Quarterly* (spring): 68-74.

GlobalSecurity.org. 2005a. Arak. Available from http://www.globalsecurity.org/wmd/ world/ iran/arak.htm. Internet. Accessed on 11 April 2005.

_____. 2005b. Bushehr. Available from http://www.globalsecurity.org/wmd/world/ iran/bushehr.htm. Internet. Accessed on 16 April 2005.

_____. 2005c. OPLAN 5027 major theater war-west: phase 3 counter attack. Available from http://globalsecurity.org/military/ops/oplan-5027-3.htm. Internet. Accessed on 1 April 2005.

_____. 2005d. North Korea-South Korea Tensions. Available from http:// globalsecurity.org/military/world/war/north_korea2.htm24. Internet. Accessed on 24 May 2005.

Graham, Bradley, and Glenn Kessler. 2005. N. Korean nuclear advance is cited. *Washington Post*. Available from https://www.us.army.mil/suite/earlybird/Apr 2005/e20050429365718.html. Internet. Accessed on 29 April 2005.

Gray, Christine. 2000. *International law and the use of force*. New York: Oxford University Press.

Harden, James D. 1997. Israeli nuclear weapons and war in the Middle East. Research Study, Naval Postgraduate School, Monterey, CA.

Hayes, Peter, 2002. The agreed framework is dead: Long live the agreed framework! *The Nautilus Institute*, 16 October. Available from http://www.nautilus.org/DPRK BriefingBook/agreedFramework/0204Peter.html. Internet. Accessed on 1 April 2005.

Herzog, Chaim. 1975. *The war of atonement October 1973*, Boston, MA: Little, Brown and Company, First American Edition.

House International Relations Committee. 1996. China's military sales to Iran. U.S. Congress, 12 September. Available from http://www.iranwatch.org/government/ US/Congress/Hearings/hirc-091296/us-hirc-chinairan-091296.htm. Internet. Accessed on 8 April 2005.

International Atomic Energy Agency. 2004. Communication dated 26 November received from the permanent representatives of France, Germany, the Islamic Republic of Iran and the United Kingdom concerning the agreement signed in Paris. Available from http://iaea.org. Internet. Accessed on 10 April 2005.

Iran hints at pre-emption over threat from U.S. *International Herald Tribune*, [20 August 2004]. Available from http://iht.com/bin/print.php?file=534819.html. Internet. Accessed on 6 December 2004.

Jewish Virtual Library. 1981. *Raid on the Iraqi reactor*. Available from http://www. jewishvirtuallibrary.org/jsource/History/Osirak.html. Internet. Accessed on 23 September, 2004.

Jones, Ronald D. 1996. Israeli air superiority in the 1967 Arab Israeli war: An analysis of operational art. Research Project, Naval War College, Newport, RI.

Katz, Mark N. 2004. Russian ruminations on the prospects of a nuclear Iran. *CDI Russia Weekly*, 7 October. Available from http://www.cdi.org/russia/325-19.cfm. Internet. Accessed on 16 April 2005.

Keegan, John. 2004. *The Iraq war*. New York, NY: Alfred A. Knopf.

Kenney, Steven L. 2004. The national security strategy under the United Nations and international law. Research Project, U.S. Army War College, Carlisle Barracks, PA.

Knox, MacGregor and Williamson Murray. *The dynamics of military revolution, 1300-2050*. New York: Cambridge University Press.

Laffin, John. 1985. *The war of desperation*. London: Osprey Publishing Ltd.

Leffler, Melvyn P. 2004. Bush's foreign policy. *Foreign Policy* (September-October): 22-28.

Lehrer, Jim, Anchor and Executive Editor, PBS. 2004. Transcript & Video: Debate #1, George Bush and John Kerry. Fox News Channel transcript of debate 30 September 2004. Available from http://www.foxnews.com/printer_friendly_story/0,3566,134152,00.html. Internet. Accessed 1 October 2004.

Lobeto, Xavier P. 2004. Strategy at war: A policy left without the means. Research Project, U.S. Army War College, Carlisle Barracks, PA.

Luvass, Jay. 1986. *Frederick the great: The education of a great captain.* In H200, *Military revolutions parallel course: From pike-squares to PGMs*, Vol. I. Fort Leavenworth, KS: US Army Command and General Staff Officers Course.

Manyin, Mark E., Emma Chanlett-Avery, and Helene Marchart. 2005. CRS Report for Congress: *North Korea: A chronology of events, October 2002-December 2004.* Available from http://www.fas.org/man/crs/rl32743.pdf. Internet. Accessed on 30 March 2005.

McBrien, John, M. 2004. The Bush doctrine: Shifting position and closing the stance. Strategic Research Project, U.S. Army War College, Carlisle Barracks, PA.

McCoubrey, Hilaire, and Nigel D. White. 1992. *International law and armed conflict.* Brookfield, VT: Ashgate Publishing Ltd.

McMahon, Robert. 2004. UN: Russian statement on preemption revives focus on UN role, 10 September. Available from http://www.rferl.org/featuresarticle/2004/09/797086a7-dcfa-41bb-8244-c527c0d1dd7c.html. Internet. Last accessed on 9 May 2005.

McMullen, Thomas C. 2004. The Bush doctrine: Power concepts, preemption, and the global war on terror. Strategic Research Project, U.S. Army War College, Carlisle Barracks, PA.

MILNET. 2004. *Iranian progress toward developing nuclear weapons.* Available from http://www.milnet.com/Iranian-Nuclear-Chronology.htm. Internet. Accessed on 3 April 2005.

Murphy, Dan. 2002. Terror-preemption talk roils Asia. *The Christian Science Monitor,* 5 December. Available from http://www.csmonitor.com/2002/1205/ p06s01-woap. html. Internet. Last accessed on 10 May 2005.

Myers, Harry L. 1997. The US policy of dual containment toward Iran and Iraq in theory and practice. Research Report, Air War College, Maxwell AFB, AL.

NMS. 2004. *See* U.S. President. 2004

NSCT. 2003. *See* U.S. President. 2003

NSS. 2002. *See* U.S. President. 2002a

Nye, Joseph S. 2003. *Understanding international conflicts: An introduction to theory and history*. New York: Longman.

O'Hanlon, Michael E, Susan E. Rice, and James B. Steinberg. 2002. Policy Brief #113, *The new national security strategy and preemption*. Brookings Institution. Available from www.brookings.edu/index/taxonomy.htm?taxonomy=Defense* Defense%20strategy*Strategic%20doctrine. Internet. Last accessed on 10 May 2005.

O'Hanlon, Michael, and Michael A. Levi. 2003. Preempting North Korean threat in the sea, 20 June. Avaliable from http://yaleglobal.yale.edu/display.article?id=1899. Internet. Accessed on 1 April 2005.

OPLAN 5027. 2005. *See* GlobalSecurity.org. 2005c.

Oren, Michael B. 2003. *Six days of war*. New York: Presidio Press.

Owens, Christopher S. 2003. Unlikely partners: Preemption and the American way of war. In *Essays*. Washington, DC: Chairman of the Joint Chiefs of Staff.

Perkovich, George. 2003. From victory to success: Can Iran and the United States bridge the gulf. *Foreign Policy*, July/August, 65. Available from http://www.foreign policy.com/story/cms.php?story_id=128&print=1. Internet. Accessed on 20 October 2004.

Perlmutter, Amos, Michael I. Handel, and Uri Bar-Joseph. 2003. *Two minutes over Baghdad*. Portland, OR: Frank Cass Publishers.

Pollack, Kenneth M., Mark Palmer, and David Kay. 2005. Transition 2005: U.S. policy toward Iran. Interview by Ray Takeyh, Council on Foreign Relations, 12 January. Available from http://www.cfr.org/pub7605/david_kay_kenneth_m_ pollack_mark_palmer_ray_takeyh/transition_2005_us_policy_toward_iran.php. Internet. Accessed on 3 April 2005.

Pollard. Mark D. 2002. Will they know it when they see it? The ill and crime of aggression. Judge Advocate General's School, Maxwell AFB, AL.

Powell, Colin, U.S. Secretary of State. 2003. Remarks to the United Nations security council, 5 February. Available from http://www.whitehouse.gov/news/releases/ 2003/02/20030205-1.html. Internet. Accessed on 25 March 2005.

Priest, Lesley S. 2003. Implications of the policy of preemption on combatant commanders. Research Project, Naval War College, Newport, RI.

Raman, B. 2003. South East Asia Analysis Group, *Iran: An Osirak in the offing*, no. 700, 29 May 2003. Available from http://www.saag.org/papers7/paper700.html. Internet. Accessed on 23 September 2004.

Record, Jeffrey. 2003. *Bounding the global war on terrorism*. Strategic Research Project, U.S. Army War College, CarlisleBarricks, PA.

Rehbein, David J. 1998. Countering the proliferation of weapons of mass destruction; the case for strategic preemption. Strategic Research Project, U.S. Army War College, Carlisle Barracks, PA.

Reuters. 2004. Iran says may preempt any attack on nuke program. Available from http://www.ufolab.info/islam.htm. Internet. Accessed on 10 September 2004.

Robertson Jr., Horace B. 1991. Specific means and methods of application of force. *Duke Journal of Comparative and International Law* 1991, no. 1. Available from http://eprints.law.duke.edu/archive/00000474/01/ 1_Duke_J._Comp._& _Int%27l_L._1_(1991).pdf. Internet. Accessed on 18 April 2005.

Robinson, George M. 2003. Deterrence and the national security strategy of 2002: A round peg for a round hole. Research Project, Naval Postgraduate School, Monterey, CA

Roots of Strategy, Book 2. [1987]. Harrisburg, PA: Stackpole Books.

Rushworth, Charles T. 1997. The theater commander's preemptive strike option against WMD. Research Project, Naval War College, Newport, RI.

Safranchuk, Ivan, Dr. *The U.S. national security strategy: A Russian perception.* Available from http://www.cdi.org/national-security/moscow.cfm. Internet. Accessed on 20 October 2004.

Sanger, David E and William J. Broad. 2005. Using clues from Libya to study a nuclear mystery, *New York Times*, 31 March.

Schmitt, Michael N. 2003a. International law and the use of force: Attacking Iraq. *Royal United Services Institute Journal* (February): 13-15

_____. 2003b. Preemptive strategies in international law. *Michigan Journal of International Law*, 24 (winter): 513-548.

Simpkin, Richard E. 1988. *Race to the swift: Thoughts on twenty-first century warfare.* Exeter, Great Britain: Brassey's Defence Publishers.

Smith, Fred. 2003. National security 'strategy: A flawed guide to the future. Industrial College of the Armed Forces, National Defense University.

Smith, Jennifer L. 2003. Unilateral preemptive self-defense, Has Its Time Arrived: Assessing the International Legality of Unilateral; Self Defense in the 2002 National Security Strategy. Research Project, The George Washington University Law School.

Smith, Michael A., and Jeffrey L. Schloesser. 1997. The preemptive use of force: Analysis and decisionmaking. Research project, Army War College, Carlisle Barracks, PA.

Sokolosi, Henry, and Patrick Clawson. ed. 2004. *Checking Iran's nuclear ambitions.* Non-Proliferation Policy Center. Available from http://www.npec-web.org/books/ CheckingIran.pdf. Internet. Accessed on 9 April 2005.

Solana, Javier. 2004. Rules with teeth. *Foreign Policy*, September-October: 74-75.

Squassoni, Sharon A., 2003. *Weapons of mass destruction: Trade between North Korea and Pakistan.* CRS Report for Congress. Available from http://www.www. fas.org/spp/starwars/crs/rl31000.pdf. Internet. Accessed on 1 April 2005.

Stoessinger, John G. 2001. *Why nations go to war,* Boston, MA: Bedford/St. Martin's.

Sullivan, Paul. 2002. US-Iran relations since 9-11: A monologue of civilizations. Alternatives. *Turkish Journal of International Relations* 1, no. 2 (Summer): 178-203.

Takahashi, Kosuke. 2005. China's worsening North Korean headache. *Asia Times*, 29 January. Available from http://www.nautilus.org/DPTK BriefingBook/china /PRC_Takahashi.html. Internet. Accessed on 1 April 2005.

Thucydides. 1972. *History of the Peloponnesian War.* New York: Penguin Books.

Torbakov, Igor. 2002. *Russia's ultimatum to Georgia appears addressed more to Washington than Tbilisi.* Available from http://www.eurasianet.org/ departments/insight/articles/eav091702a.shtml. Internet. Accessed on 24 May 2005.

U.S. Department of State. 2004. *Background note: New Zealand*, September. Available from http://www.stat.gov/r/pa/ei/bgn/35852.htm. Internet. Accessed on 24 May 2005

U.S. House of Representative, Committee on International Relations. 2004. Implications of a nuclear Iran, June. Available from http://wwwc.house.gov/international_ relations/108/eis062404.htm. Internet. Accessed on 3 April 2005.

U.S. President. 2002. West Point Graduation Speech, 1 June. Available from http://www.whitehouse.gov/news/releases/2002/06/ print/20020601-3.html. Internet. Accessed on 21 September 2004.

_____. 2002a. *National security strategy of the United States of America.* Washington, DC: Government Printing Office.

_____. 2002b. *National strategy to combat weapons of mass destruction.* Washington, DC. Government Printing Office.

_____. 2003. *NSCT.* Washington, DC: Government Printing Office.

_____. 2004. *National military strategy of the United States of America.* Washington, DC: Government Printing Office.

_____. 2005. *Notice: Continuation of the national emergency with respect to Iran,* March. Available from http://www.whitehouse.gov/news/releases/2005/03/ 20050310-9.html. Internet. Accessed on 3 April 2005.

Valasek, Tomas. 2002. *The U.S. national security strategy: A view from Europe.* Available from http://www.cdi.org/national-security/brussels.cfm. Internet. Accessed on 20 October 2004.

Vasta, Robert J. 2004. Are preemptive attacks morally bankrupt? Strategic Research Project, U.S. Army War College, Carlisle Barracks, PA.

Walzer, Michael. 2000. *Just and unjust wars.* 3rd ed. New York, NY: Basic Books.

Weismann, Steven R. 2003. Preemption: Idea with a lineage whose time has come. *New York Times,* 23 March. Available from http://www.mtholyoke.edu/acad/intrel/ bush/preempt.htm. Internet. Accessed on 21 September 2004.

Woodward, Bob. 2004. *Plan of attack.* New York, NY: Simon and Schuster.

Yaphe, Judith. 2002. *U.S.-Iran relations: Normalization in the future?* Strategic Forum Number 188, January. Available from http://www.ndu.edu/inss/strforum/h6.html. Internet. Accessed on 9 April.

Ziemke, Caroline F. 2001. *Strategic personality and the effectiveness of nuclear deterrence: Deterring Iraq and Iran.* Alexandria, VA: Institute for Defense Analyses.

Zinni, Anthony General Ret, USMC. 2004. Remarks at Center for Defense Information Board of Director's dinner, 12 May. Available at http://www.cdi.org/friendly version/printversion.cfm?documentID=2208. Internet. Accessed on 25 March 2005.